FAST FACTS®
ON THE
MASONIC
LODGE

John Ankerberg
& John Weldon

HARVEST HOUSE PUBLISHERS

EUGENE, OREGON

Cover by Terry Dugan Design, Minneapolis, Minnesota

FAST FACTS® ON THE MASONIC LODGE
Updated and revised from *Christianity and the Secret Teachings of the Masonic Lodge;* includes some material from *The Facts on the Masonic Lodge*
Copyright © 2004 by John Ankerberg and John Weldon
Published by Harvest House Publishers
Eugene, Oregon 97402
www.harvesthousepublishers.com

Harvest House Publishers, Inc., is the exclusive licensee of the federally registered trademark FAST FACTS.

Library of Congress Cataloging-in-Publication Data

Ankerberg, John, 1945-
  Fast facts on the Masonic lodge / John Ankerberg and John Weldon.
      p. cm.
Includes bibliographical references.
  ISBN 0-7369-1343-2 (pbk.)
  1. Freemasonry—Religious aspects—Christianity. 2. Freemasonry—United States. I. Weldon, John. II. Title.
  HS495.A55 2004
  366'.1—dc22

                                        2003024195

Printed in the United States of America

04 05 06 07 08 09 10 11 12 / BP-MS / 10 9 8 7 6 5 4 3 2 1

CONTENTS

Section IV: The Bible of Masonry

Section V: The God of Masonry

SECTION VI: MASONRY AND JESUS CHRIST

SECTION VII: MASONRY AND CHRISTIANS

For Donald McClintock, Robb Finberg,
and Darrel Runches

*Freemasonry stands for the values that are
supreme in the life of the church and expects each
member to follow his own faith and to place his duty
to God above all other duties. We are sure that a member
who is true to the principles he learns in Freemasonry
will be a better church member because of it (206).*

—"Freemasonry and Religion,"
Grand Lodge of British Columbia and Yukon Web site

THE IMPORTANCE OF UNDERSTANDING WHAT MASONRY REALLY TEACHES

The purpose of this book is to compare the teachings of Christianity with those of the Masonic Lodge.

For some 200 years Masonry has influenced the Christian church in North America. Today, such influence is perhaps greater than ever before. In 1993, an arm of the largest Protestant denomination in the United States, the Southern Baptist Convention, concluded that Christian membership in the Lodge was simply "a matter of personal conscience." This conclusion remains accepted by the SBC more than a decade later (185).* Notably, it has proven to have invigorated Freemasonry in its relationship to Christianity and warranted Lodge membership in the minds of many Christians (see appendix B for further discussion).

The reason Masonry continues to find an influence within the Church is due to both the nature of the claims made in Masonry and the fact that both Christians and Masons are often unaware of the true spiritual teachings and implications of Masonry.

This volume has been written out of concern for both parties—but especially for Masons who are Christians. Once what Masonry really teaches becomes clear, a great deal of the misunderstanding over this subject is dissipated. If you are a Christian (especially one with friends or relatives in Masonry), a Christian Mason, or simply curious about what the Lodge really teaches, this book is for you.

---

* Reference information throughout this book is found in parentheses. It includes the bibliography number found in the back of this book and the referenced page number(s) in the work cited. Multiple sources are separated by semicolons. Where a source has more than one volume, the volume number is identified with a Roman numeral.

A Word to Masons

Today the Masonic Lodge has over two million members worldwide, who look to Masonry for the brotherhood and fellowship it has brought into their lives. These members believe they are part of an organization engaged in worthwhile causes, such as supporting children's hospitals, and they feel strongly about the Masonic "landmarks," or doctrines, concerning the fatherhood of God, the brotherhood of man, and the immortality of the soul. We can certainly acknowledge the good that Masons have done in the world through their philanthropic endeavors, so a Mason might wonder, how then can we have concerns about Masonry?

Our concerns are motivated by the fact that we care about Masons and honor and respect individual Masons as fellow human beings, made in the image of God. We care about them as people for whom Christ died. Because Jesus commanded us as Christians to go into all the world and preach the gospel—and because the apostles instructed Christians to earnestly contend for the faith (Jude 3)—we have not only written this book comparing biblical teaching with Masonic ritual and belief, but we have also written books comparing biblical teaching with the literature of the Watchtower Society (Jehovah's Witnesses), the Church of Jesus Christ of Latter-day Saints (Mormonism), and other religious or secular persuasions.

As with these other organizations, it is the nature of the truth claims made by the Masonic Lodge we have taken issue with, not individual Masons. We feel it is our obligation to do this, both for the sake of Masons and for those who might become Masons. After all, Masonry and its relationship to Christian faith have caused controversy for more than 200 years. This means at least two things: 1) Different sides have taken different positions on various issues and have attempted to defend their positions to the best of their ability; 2) therefore, confusion is likely for the layperson, who has to carefully wade through the arguments on both sides before he can hope to resolve the issue responsibly. Our aim is to compare and clarify these positions.

Finally, we wish to remind the reader that to argue with a philosophy is not to reject the value or importance of the person who holds that philosophy. The apostle Peter commanded all Christians, "In your hearts set apart Christ as Lord. Always be prepared to give an answer to everyone who asks you to give the reason for the hope that you have. But do this with gentleness and respect..." (1 Peter 3:15 NIV).

INTRODUCTION TO MASONRY

As a fraternity, we are always ready to be judged—
severely and critically (101:1).
—Francis G. Paul, Thirty-Third-Degree
Sovereign Grand Commander

1

WHAT IS MASONRY AND HOW INFLUENTIAL IS IT?

Masonry (also known as Freemasonry, or "the Lodge") is a powerful, 2-million-member, centuries-old fraternal order that began in the early eighteenth century. According to most Masonic authorities, modern Masonry (also called *speculative* Masonry) can be traced to the founding of the first Grand Lodge in London in A.D. 1717 (70,I:131,152; 1:3; 15:12).

The Lodge is also a secret society. To maintain its secrets, Masonry uses symbolism, secret oaths, and secret rituals to instruct new members, who are called *initiates*. Each new member swears during these secret ceremonies to remain loyal to the Lodge and its teachings. The teachings instruct each new candidate how he is to serve God and his fellow man and tell him of the rewards he can expect. The symbols of Masonry are the actual tools of the old stonecutters and builders, such as the gavel, compass, plumb, square, and level, which are employed to inculcate moral and religious lessons.

Definitions

Let us examine the definition of Masonry as given by Masons themselves. Albert Mackey, in his *Revised Encyclopedia of Freemasonry,* asserts "All [Masons] unite in declaring it to be a system of morality, by the practice of which its members may advance their spiritual interest, and mount by the theological ladder from the Lodge on earth to the Lodge in heaven" (96,I:269).

Additional authoritative definitions are as follows:

> It is a science which is engaged in the search after Divine Truth, and which employs symbolism as its method of instruction (96,I:269).

> [Masonry is] that religious and mystical society whose aim is moral perfection on the basis of general equality and fraternity (96,I:269).

> Freemasonry, in its broadest and most comprehensive sense, is a system of morality and social ethics, a primitive religion, and a philosophy of life,...incorporating a broad humanitarianism;...it is a religion without a creed, being of no sect but finding truth in all;...it seeks truth but does not define truth (36:234).

> A man who becomes a Mason is defined by Masonic authorities as being "one who has been initiated into the mysteries of the fraternity of Freemasonry" (96,I:378).

What we present in this book is an analysis of Masonry itself, as laid out by Masonic authorities recommended to us by half of the Grand Lodges in the United States (see question 2). The Grand Lodge of each state (and the District of Columbia) sets the ritual and the interpretation of that ritual that is to be followed by the members of that state. Although each Grand Lodge is the final authority for each state, a comparison shows little difference overall either in the ritual or in the interpretation of the ritual, though placement of materials may vary (182).

Masonry's Influence

The influence of Masonry remains considerable despite significant losses in membership over the last few decades, and declining influence and prestige. Membership has declined from four million (in the period from 1952 to 1970) to about 2 to 2.5 million today (1.7 million in the U.S.)—although this may not include a significant membership in the many appendant organizations (183). According to the most recent statistics available (June 2001), Masonry retains about 22,000 lodges in some 70 countries. Of 192 countries in the world, almost 40 percent have Masonic Grand Lodges (184). In addition, there are literally thousands of Masonic Web sites (some 1,700 Masonic and appendant sites are listed at the "E-M@son Link System," and thousands of Masonic sites are also listed at two other megasites) (187).

In *Behind the Lodge Door*, Paul A. Fisher, who has a background in military and other intelligence, asserts that Masonry has "enormous influence in the world media" and that it influenced or dominated the U.S. Supreme Court for more than 30 years. The ratio (Masons to non-Masons) was 5 to 4 (1941–46), 8 to 1 (1949–56), 6 to 3 (1957–67), and 5 to 4 (1969–71) (121:1-17, 242-44, 260-68). According to one Lodge history compiled by Paul Bessel, Executive Secretary of the Masonic Leadership Center, from 1789 to 1992 about one-third of the Supreme Court Justices have apparently been Masons. (However, from 1992 to the present, for the first time there is apparently not a single Mason sitting on the Court.) (188)

According to Masonic sources, as many as 14 U.S. presidents have been Masons, and 14 vice presidents as well. According to the Senate Congressional Record of September 9, 1987, Masons constituted 41 members of the federal judiciary, 50 percent of the Senate Judiciary Committee, 18 senators, and 76 members of the House of Representatives. Among the famous and influential of the world, the Masonic list reads like a who's who: Sir Winston Churchill, W.C. Fields, Henry Ford, Norman Vincent Peale, Luther Burbank, Benjamin Franklin, Barry Goldwater, J. Edgar Hoover, Rudyard Kipling, Charles Lindbergh, General Douglas MacArthur,

Peter Marshall, Johann Wolfgang von Goethe, Roy Rogers, all seven of the Ringling Brothers, and too many others to list (189).

2

WHAT IS THE FINAL AUTHORITY FOR THE TEACHINGS PRESENTED IN EACH MASONIC LODGE?

If anyone is going to investigate the teachings of the Masonic Lodge, who or what is the accepted authority they should listen to? When, on our television program, we asked this question of Mr. Bill Mankin, a thirty-second-degree Mason, he said, "The authoritative source for Masonry is the ritual. The ritual—what happens in the Lodge, what goes on" (1:3,5).

When one examines Masonry and compares the different manuals containing the ritual for each state (these textbooks are called *monitors*), it is apparent that, at least today, the ritual and the interpretations given are very close. As former Worshipful Master Jack Harris comments, "In other states...the principle and the doctrines [of the ritual] are exactly the same. The wording only varies slightly" (13:29). Therefore, the ritual in the monitors can be considered the authoritative teachings of the Lodge.

But we also wanted to know which authors and books Masons themselves recommend to outsiders as authoritative. In order to answer this question, we sent a letter to each of the 51 Grand Lodges in America. The letter was addressed to the Grand Master of each, asking him to respond to the following question: "As an official Masonic leader, which books and authors do you recommend as being authoritative on the subject of Freemasonry?" Twenty-five of the 51 Grand Lodges in the United States responded.* (Remember, for each state there is no higher authority than its Grand Lodge.)

---

* Arizona, Colorado, Connecticut, Delaware, District of Columbia, Idaho, Illinois, Indiana, Iowa, Kansas, Louisiana, Maine, Massachusetts, Mississippi, Missouri, New Jersey, New Mexico, New York, Ohio, Pennsylvania, South Carolina, Texas, Utah, Virginia, Wisconsin.

3

WHICH BOOKS AND AUTHORS HAVE BEEN RECOMMENDED BY THE GRAND LODGES AS BEING AUTHORITATIVE INTERPRETERS FOR MASONRY?

These are the sources that the Grand Lodges most often recommended in their replies to our letter (see question 2):

- 44%—Henry Wilson Coil, *Coil's Masonic Encyclopedia*

- 36%—Joseph Fort Newton, *The Builders*

- 32%—Albert G. Mackey, *Mackey's Revised Encyclopedia of Freemasonry*

- 24%—Carl H. Claudy, *Introduction to Freemasonry*

- 24%—H.L. Haywood, *The Newly-Made Mason*

- 20%—Alphonse Cerza, *A Masonic Reader's Guide*

- 20%—Robert F. Gould, *History of Freemasonry*

- 20%—Allen E. Roberts, *The Craft and Its Symbols*

- 16%—Albert Pike, *Morals and Dogma**

The responses reveal that Coil, Newton, and Mackey are the three leading Masonic authorities (see 49:172; 57:8,148; 51,I:130). Because of the high esteem in which these authors are held by the Grand Lodges, we will often document our analysis of Masonry from their texts. At the same time, we have not neglected the other Masonic authors recommended by the Grand Lodges. Masons should acknowledge that these authors and books do represent their most authoritative interpreters of Freemasonry.

---

* Other authors recommended included W.R. Denslow, R.V. Denslow, Charles C. Hunt, Bernard Jones, Roscoe Pound, James Anderson, Henry Clausen, D. Darrah, Manly P. Hall, W. Hutchinson, M.M. Johnson, Karl C.F. Krause, W. Preston, G. Steinmetz, J.H. Van Gorden, T.S. Webb, and Louis Williams.

4

What Are the Blue Lodge, the Scottish Rite, and the York Rite, and What Other Organizations Are Associated with Masonry?

All men who become Masons go through the Blue Lodge, the parent or mother Lodge of Freemasonry. In the Blue Lodge are conferred the first three degrees: 1) the Entered Apprentice, in which a man is initiated into the beginning mysteries of the fraternity of Freemasonry; 2) the degree of Fellow Craft; and 3) the Master Mason degree. After passing these three degrees in the Blue Lodge, the candidate may choose not to proceed further at all, or he may choose to proceed higher along one or both of two branches.

One branch is known as the Scottish Rite, which advances by numerical degrees, beginning with the fourth and ending with the thirty-second, the thirty-third degree being either active or honorary. The other major branch is the York Rite, which names its degrees, going through what is called the "Chapter," "Council," and "Commandery" degrees and ending with the degree of Knights Templar.

If a Mason is suspended or expelled from his Blue Lodge, it automatically severs his connection from all other Masonic bodies. Anyone who passes the first three degrees and becomes a Master Mason may visit other Blue Lodges than his own.

On the opposite page we present a diagram of the three Blue Lodge degrees plus the optional degrees of the York and Scottish Rites (74; see 100).

Other Masonic Organizations

Besides the degrees noted in our diagram, there are many affiliated, appendant organizations or side degrees of Masonry, which to varying extents support Masonry. These are orders with specific memberships or goals. Some of these include the Order of the Eastern Star for the wives, daughters, and other female relatives of

Blue Lodge Degrees and
Optional York and Scottish Rites

Blue Lodge
1. Entered Apprentice
2. Fellow Craft
3. Master Mason

York Rite	Scottish Rite
Chapter (capitular degrees)	*Lodge of Perfection*
Mark Master	4. Secret Master
	5. Perfect Master
	6. Intimate Secretary
Past Master (Virtual)	7. Provost & Judge
	8. Intendant of the Building
	9. Elu of the Nine
	10. Elu of the Fifteen
Most Excellent Master	11. Elu of the Twelve
	12. Master Architect
	13. Royal Arch of Solomon
Royal Arch Mason	14. Perfect Elu
Council (cryptic degrees)	*Chapter Rose Croix*
	15. Knight of the East or Sword
	16. Prince of Jerusalem
Royal Master	17. Knight of the East & West
	18. Knight Rose Croix
	Council of Kadosh
	19. Grand Pontiff
Select Master	20. Master of the Symbolic Lodge
	21. Noachite or Prussian Knight
	22. Knight of the Royal Axe
Super Excellent Master	23. Chief of the Tabernacle
	24. Prince of the Tabernacle
Commandery (chivalric degrees)	25. Knight of the Brazen Serpent
Order of the Red Cross	26. Prince of Mercy
	27. Knight Commander of the Temple
	28. Knight of the Sun
Order of the Knights of Malta	29. Knight of St. Andrew
	30. Knight Kadosh
	Consistory
	31. Inspector Inquisitor
Order of Knights Templar	32. Master of the Royal Secret
Commandery	33. (Active or Honorary)

Master Masons; the Shriners (the Ancient Arabic Order of Nobles of the Mystic Shrine—the Shriners are linked to Arabic traditions, and only thirty-second-degree Masons and Knights Templar are eligible for membership); the Order of DeMolay (a boys' fraternity); Job's Daughters (for young women); Daughters of the Nile (for women relatives of Shriners); the Mystic Order of Veiled Prophets of the Enchanted Realm (the Grotto, a social organization); Acacia Fraternity (for collegians); Knights of the Red Cross of Constantine (an order of six degrees whose members must be Royal Arch Masons); and many others (19:18-22,48-59). According to Paul Bessel, Executive Secretary of the Masonic Leadership Center, there are some 50 national appendant bodies in the U.S. (207).

Several of the appendant organizations exist to introduce the sons, daughters, wives, and other relatives of Masons to a basic Masonic worldview—with the assumed understanding that the Mason himself as head of the household might fill in any remaining gaps. In this sense, these organizations function as an introduction into Masonry, one designed to support the Mason himself by ensuring that his personal environment (mother, wife, children, and others) becomes a support and encouragement for his Masonic involvement.

For example, rudimentary Masonic beliefs can be seen in the ritual for the *Order of the Eastern Star.* Dr. Rob Morris, a leading Mason, is considered the "Master Builder" of the Order. In the ritual, emphasis is laid upon 1) faith in [the Masonic] God; 2) secrecy and solemn oaths; and 3) personal character-building and the immortality of the soul. However, as is typical in the appendant organizations, these beliefs are not as forcefully or clearly stated as in the rituals of Masonry itself (for example, 181:77), and they may be absent.

Masonic Organizations for Youth

The founder of the *Order of DeMolay* (membership about 20,000), Frank Land, is described as "a devoted champion of

Freemasonry and of its teachings, [who] would become a figure of international prominence within Masonry" (190). The originator of the DeMolay ritual, Frank Marshall, believed "Almighty God" had inspired him to prepare it in 1919. "Perhaps my greatest task in the beginning was to avoid Masonic phraseology, for in the pioneer days the fear of copying Masonry was a very real one and there was a very definite opposition to anything that suggested any connection with Masonry or that DeMolay should appear as a preparation for future Masons" (190). Nevertheless, Masonic authority Carl Claudy noted,

> I believe that most boys, when they grow up to be men, will turn from the elaborate and spectacular degrees of the DeMolay Order to the more quiet, thoughtful and deeper degrees of Masonry with relief, and will throw themselves in them with greater enthusiasm....No boy who has been a DeMolay will ever join a Masonic lodge without being better prepared to become a good Mason (191).

The *International Order of Job's Daughters,* which currently has 20,000 members, "is religious in nature" and requires every member to have a relationship to a Master Mason. Membership "is to be composed of developing girls who believe in God and bear a Masonic relationship" (192).

Commenting on these bodies, one authority notes,

> The three Masonic youth organizations are the International Order of DeMolay, the International Order of Job's Daughters, and the International Order of Rainbow for Girls. What a great story of how the Masonic family has grown because of these three organizations. The three people who started these organizations over 70 years ago have increased the Masonic family by tens of thousands. These three people never asked a man to become a Mason, but because of their impact, tens of thousands of men have petitioned Masonry (193).

5

WHAT ARE THE DIFFERENT LEVELS OF SPIRITUAL ENLIGHTENMENT IN MASONRY?

We note three basic "groupings" of Masons:

1. The Nominally Religious Mason

This Mason has been through the rites stressing the importance of Masonic religion, but he has turned Masonry into merely a social club and a secular brotherhood. For him, Masonry is a means to social standing and advancement or a means to assist his business or employment through contacts with other Masons. He is content in his view of Masonry as it is. One ten-year study concluded, "The average Mason is largely ignorant of Masonic teachings....The fact is that the overwhelming majority of Masons hardly ever attend Lodge and are ignorant of the availability of Masonic books....Theology is the last thing on their minds when they first consider becoming Masons" (168:1-2). For this Mason, the entire subject of religion is largely irrelevant, and the standard arguments that Masonry is not a religion seem more than convincing. Many, perhaps most, of these Masons have not even read their own monitors.

However, some Masons see a trend within Masonry toward the next two categories.

2. The Humanistically Religious Mason

This Mason accepts, lives, and promotes the religious nature of Masonry—but largely at its face value. He accepts the literal, or "outer," meaning of Masonry. He is committed to Masonic truth as he sees it and seeks to live his life according to Masonic ideals: the fatherhood of God, the brotherhood of man, the immortality of the soul, and Masonry as the hope of the future. This Mason would view the first category of Mason as a "backslider" who has dishonored the sacred truths of Masonry.

For this Mason, the *claims* of Masonry about religion are key—for example, that Masonry seeks true religious brotherhood in which men of all faiths may unite in common worship of the one true God, which will hopefully lead to a common universal brotherhood. He believes that he can logically accept the faith of Masonry and also practice his own religion, whatever it is, and that Masonry will provide greater meaning and depth for his personal beliefs. He does not consider the matter further and therefore never understands the true nature of Masonry.

The Mason at this level has still not understood Masonry. Within this grouping we could place Christian Masonry, which would include the hundreds of thousands of Christians in Masonry, especially in the South of the United States.

But in order to truly understand Masonry, we must examine the third grouping.

3. The Mystically Religious Mason

This Mason looks at Masonry at a deeper and more esoteric level. He finds in it a thoroughgoing system of mysticism, even offering occult enlightenment for those who seek it. He sees almost everything in Masonry as part of the tradition of the ancient mystery schools, as a gnostic religion whose "outer form" ("grouping 2 above") preserves the genuine secrets of true Masonry from the profane (that is, the unenlightened, whether Mason or non-Mason). Even in the Blue Lodge "a double meaning is attached to these symbols and art speech...which very few apprehend" (16:142; see 16:143;147-48,150,162).

This Mason views Masons in the first two groupings as ignorant or naïve—they are unenlightened as to the real nature of Masonry. For this Mason, Masonry is the one true religion, whose mystical core constitutes the inner truths of all religions.*

This understanding of Masonry explains why so many leading Masons contend that other Masons live in spiritual ignorance.

---

* Although this category is discussed herein, a much fuller exposition can be found in our book *The Secret Teachings of the Masonic Lodge*, part four (Moody Press, 1990).

Consider the following authoritative statements by Masons (including one former Mason):

- Allen E. Roberts comments, "There is much that is still unknown to even the ardent Masonic student" (79:6).

- Rollin C. Blackmer complains, "It is a lamentable fact that the great mass of our membership are...densely ignorant of everything connected with Masonry" (50:1).

- An official Masonic text acknowledges, "The majority of Masons are sadly lacking in the knowledge of the height, breadth and depth of Masonic teachings contained in the meanings of the many symbols of Masonry" (92:65).

- Former Mason Edmond Ronayne maintains that "those who know the least about Freemasonry are the Masons themselves" (31:242).

- The Reverend William H. Russell declares that "nearly every Mason thinks he knows all about Masonry, and also what Speculative [modern] Masonry is. As a matter of fact, however, he does not" (14:7).

- George H. Steinmetz concludes, "Most of the truly great Masonic writers have deplored the lack of esoteric Masonic knowledge among the Craft in general....The average Mason is lamentably ignorant of the real meaning of Masonic Symbology and knows as little of its esoteric teaching" (43:2,5).

- After almost ten years of research into Masonry (168:xi), Steven Tsoukalas also concluded, "The average Mason is not aware of the spiritual import of the Craft degrees" (168:129).

What all this means is that the average Mason is probably unaware of the true inner meaning of Masonry—even that in the Blue Lodge practices and teachings—not to mention unacquainted with the more mystical teachings in the higher degrees.

MASONRY AND THE PLAN OF SALVATION

*Masonry is compatible with Christianity
and other Religions (165).*

—THE MASONIC INFORMATION CENTER

*Freemasonry has always been a bulwark for religious liberty. It
is a supporter of all religions. Freemasonry is not a permit for a
Mason to replace his church, but to enforce it. It does not supplant
but supplements. It does not subvert, but supports (120:7).*

—THE MASONIC GRAND CHAPLAIN OF PENNSYLVANIA

6

DOES THE MASONIC LODGE TEACH ITS MEMBERS A NONBIBLICAL PLAN OF SALVATION?

The text of the official Masonic ritual for the state of Tennessee offers the following opening prayer for those entering the First, or "Entered Apprentice," degree of Masonry. (Generally, as noted, from state by state the rituals vary only slightly.)

> Most merciful God, Supreme Architect of heaven and earth, we beseech Thee to guide and protect these brethren.... Teach us to know and serve Thee aright. Bless and prosper us in all our laudable undertakings, and grant, O God, that

our conduct may tend to Thy glory, to the advancement of
Freemasonry, and *finally to our own salvation in that blessed
kingdom* where the righteous shall find rest. Amen (65:1,
emphasis added).

Attaining one's own salvation by personal righteousness and
good works is taught throughout the entire Masonic system of
ritual and belief. Masonry not only teaches this in its prayers, but
in each of the first three degrees, in its funeral service, in all its
monitors, and also by direct statement or implication in all of its
higher degrees as well.

7

Do the Beginning Degrees of the Masonic Lodge Teach Salvation by Works?

In each of the Blue Lodge degrees, the candidate is promised by
the Lodge that God will reward him if he does good deeds and
improves his character. To demonstrate that Masonry teaches a
"works salvation" in each of its first three degrees, we only need
read the standard monitors. (We have personally examined many
monitors for different states.)

The First Degree of the Blue Lodge

Beginning with the Entered Apprentice degree, Masonry uses
the symbol of the lambskin apron to impress upon the candidate
the following instruction:

> In all ages the lamb has been deemed an emblem of inno-
> cence; he, therefore, who wears the Lambskin as a badge of
> Masonry is continually reminded of that *purity of life and
> conduct which is necessary* to obtain admittance into the
> Celestial Lodge above [Masonry's term for the afterlife],
> where the Supreme Architect of the Universe* [God] pre-
> sides (65:17, emphasis added).

---

* The Masonic deity is also called the "Great Architect of the Universe" or the "Grand Architect of the Universe." As will be seen throughout this book, these terms are often abbreviated
as *G.A.O.T.U.* or *T.G.A.O.T.U.*

No state excludes the instruction concerning the lambskin. Notably, faith in Christ is never mentioned as a requirement for Heaven, only personal conduct. Thus, although this instruction is important to the Masonic Lodge, the Bible rejects it. The Scriptures teach that our best righteousness is insuficient before God and that eternal life comes only through faith in Christ,

> All of us have become like one who is unclean, and all our righteous deeds are like a filthy garment; and all of us wither like a leaf, and our iniquities, like the wind, take us away (Isaiah 64:6).

> This is the testimony: God has given us eternal life, and this life is in his Son. He who has the Son has life; he who does not have the Son of God does not have life (1 John 5:11-12 NIV).

The Second Degree of the Blue Lodge

In the second, or "Fellow Craft," degree of Masonry, the ritual imparts the following:

> The apron of a Mason is intended to remind him of purity of mind and morals....Thus you will wear your apron while laboring among us as a speculative Fellow Craft, to distinguish you from the Entered Apprentices, ever remembering that you are to wear it as an emblem of that *purity of heart and conscience that is necessary to obtain for you the approval* of the Grand Architect of the Universe (65:41, emphasis added).

Once again the candidate is impressed with the necessity of good works to earn God's favor. But how can a Mason gain God's approval by the "purity of his heart and conscience" when the Bible offers no hope in this area?

> The heart is deceitful above all things and beyond cure. Who can understand it? I the LORD search the heart and examine the mind (Jeremiah 17:9-10).

> There is no one righteous, not even one (Romans 3:10).

Can any Mason believe he will stand before the gaze of the infinitely holy God, who searches all hearts perfectly (Leviticus 19:2; 1 Samuel 2:2; 6:20; Isaiah 57:15), and be granted the right to heaven on the basis of his own purity? What have Masons done to rid themselves of those blots on their record from when they did not live right? If the Bible reveals that God sees men as sinners who need a Savior, how will they be allowed into heaven without that Savior? Of man's standing before God, the Bible says,

> All have sinned and fall short of the glory of God (Romans 3:23).

> As it is written: "There is no one righteous, not even one" (Romans 3:10 NIV).

This is why Christ died on our behalf—because we could not save ourselves.

> "You see, at just the right time, when we were still powerless, Christ died for the ungodly....God demonstrates his own love for us in this: While we were still sinners, Christ died for us" (Romans 5:6,8 NIV).

Therefore,

> We know very well that we are not set right with God by rule keeping but only through personal faith in Jesus Christ....Convinced that no human being can please God by self-improvement, we believed in Jesus...so that we might be set right before God by trusting in [Him], not by trying to be good (Galatians 2:15-17 THE MESSAGE).

The Third Degree of the Blue Lodge

In the third Master Mason degree, the Lodge promises each candidate that, at his death, God will reward him with heavenly rewards on the basis of his "conduct," "deeds," "thoughts," and "the record of his whole life and actions." The candidate is told that, when he dies, the white linen (which he gained in the ritual of the first degree) will finally be placed upon his own coffin. Until he dies, of the apron he is to remember this:

> Let its pure and spotless surface be to you an ever present reminder of purity of life and rectitude of conduct, a never ending argument for nobler deeds, for higher thoughts, for greater achievements. And when those weary feet shall come to the end of their toilsome journey, and from your nerveless grasp shall drop forever the working tools of life, *may the record of your whole life and actions* be as pure and spotless as the fair emblem I have placed in your hands tonight. *And when at that last great day* your poor, trembling soul stands naked and alone before the great white throne, may it be your portion to hear from Him who sitteth as the Judge Supreme the welcome words, "Well done, good and faithful servant, *enter thou into the joy of thy Lord*" (65:60, emphasis added).

When a Mason dies, at his funeral service the lodge tells his family and friends his soul has gone to heaven to reside in the "Celestial Lodge Above." Even though it is admitted that the man did not live a perfect life, the Lodge confidently states that he has been accepted into heaven based on his willingness to live by the truths and principles of Masonry, expressed by his apron, which he now wears in his coffin. During the Lodge member's life it constantly reminded him of the necessity of his living a pure life and doing good deeds if he wanted to be accepted into heaven (but again Masonry never told him that faith in Christ was needed):

> Masonry has come down from the far past. It uses the tools of the builders' trade as emblems and symbols to teach Masons how to build character and moral stature....It seeks constantly to build the temple of the soul and thus to fit us for that house not made with hands, eternal in the heavens....
>
> Masons believe sincerely that when life on earth comes to a close, the soul is translated from the imperfections of this mortal sphere, to that all-perfect, glorious and Celestial Lodge Above, where God, the Grand Architect of the Universe, presides. With these truths and convictions, our brother was well acquainted.

Though perfection of character is not of this world, yet we are persuaded that our brother sought to live by these truths and principles of Masonry....

When our brother labored with us in Masonic attire, he wore a white apron, which he was taught is an emblem of innocence and a badge of a Mason. By it, he was constantly reminded of that *purity of life and that rectitude of conduct so necessary to his gaining admission into the Celestial Lodge Above.* He will now wear that apron forever as the emblem of the virtues [that is, good works] it represents....In accordance with our custom, I now place this evergreen over the heart of our brother (13:30-31, emphasis added).

Biblically speaking, on what basis can the Masonic Lodge tell Masons what God will do when they die? By what authority does the Lodge confidently assert to all who are listening that they will enter into God's presence and be accepted because of their good works, apart from faith in Christ? Is it the Bible? One of the most important places for the name of Jesus Christ to be mentioned is in a funeral service; nevertheless "these assorted Masonic [funeral] services clearly evidence the expunging of Christ from the biblical text and the wrenching of biblical texts from their proper contexts" (168:119).

8

What Is the Biblical Response to Masonic Teaching?

As we have seen, the plain teaching of the first three degrees of the Blue Lodge is that men are saved to heaven by their personal righteousness and merit. The Scripture clearly teaches the Masonic teachings on salvation are wrong at this point:

We...know that a man is not justified by observing the law, but by faith in Jesus Christ. So we, too, have put our faith in Christ Jesus that we may be justified by faith in Christ and not by observing the law, because by observing the law no one will be justified....I do not set aside the grace of God, for if righteousness could be gained through the law, Christ died for nothing! (Galatians 2:15,16,21).

Where, then, is boasting? It is excluded....For we maintain that a man is justified by faith apart from observing the law....David says the same thing when he speaks of the blessedness of the man to whom God credits righteousness apart from works (Romans 3:27-28; 4:6 NIV).

He [God] saved us, not on the basis of deeds which we have done in righteousness, but according to His mercy, by the washing of regeneration and renewing by the Holy Spirit (Titus 3:5).

By grace you have been saved, through faith—and this not from yourselves, it is the gift of God—not by works, so that no one can boast (Ephesians 2:8-9 NIV).

None will deny that a committed Mason is zealous for the "Great Architect of the Universe." But even more were the Israelites of the apostle Paul's time zealous for God. Notice, however, what the apostle said about those Israelites who sought to establish their own righteousness by doing good works:

Brothers, my heart's desire and prayer to God for the Israelites is that they may be saved. For I can testify about them that they are zealous for God, but their zeal is not based on knowledge. Since they did not know the righteousness that comes from God and sought to establish their own, they did not submit to God's righteousness (Romans 10:1-3 NIV).

The Bible is clear that a doctrine of salvation by personal merit, goodness, and works is opposed to the will of God. Rather, salvation is by grace—the free gift of God—provided when Christ died and paid the penalty for our sins:

If [salvation is] by grace, then it is no longer by works; if it were, grace would no longer be grace (Romans 11:6 NIV).

> All who rely on observing the law are under a curse, for it is written: "Cursed is everyone who does not continue to do everything written in the Book of the Law." Clearly no one is justified before God by the law, because, "The righteous will live by faith" (Galatians 3:10-11 NIV).

The Bible teaches that the only way to enter into right standing with God is by placing our complete faith in His Son, Jesus Christ. Total reliance on Jesus, admitting and turning from sin, results in *justification*. Justification means that God Himself actually declares us perfectly righteous before Him solely on the basis of our believing on Jesus and our acceptance of Him as Savior and Lord of our lives. Because of what Christ accomplished on the cross—His death having paid the penalty for our sin—God is now able to offer salvation as an entirely free gift. This means salvation is not something that can be earned, which Masonry teaches—for when has a gift ever been *earned?*

Further, when believers are declared righteous by God (Christ's perfect righteousness having been *imputed,* or reckoned, to their account), God freely forgives them of all their sins—past, present, and future. That's why the apostle can write that all believers "are justified freely by his grace through the redemption that came by Christ Jesus" (Romans 3:24), and that "in him we have redemption through his blood, the forgiveness of sins, in accordance with the riches of God's grace that he lavished on us with all wisdom and understanding" (Ephesians 1:7-8), and, "He forgave us *all* our sins" (Colossians 2:13).

9

WHAT DO AUTHORITATIVE MASONIC LITERATURE AND FORMER MASONS ACKNOWLEDGE ABOUT THE LODGE AND SALVATION?

The Masonic Lodge rebuffs all the Scriptures listed in the previous question and promises Masons that their own righteousness will save them and make them acceptable before God in heaven. For example, in the *Standard Masonic Monitor,* all Masons are taught that the *All-Seeing Eye* is a symbol for God, and that this

> All-Seeing Eye...pervades the inmost recesses of the human Heart, and will reward us according to our merits (54:111).

This monitor also teaches that the Mason is to be devoted to attaining this merit before God:

> Let all the energies of our souls and the perfection of our minds be employed in attaining the approbation [approval] of the Grand Master on high, so that when we come to die,...we gain the favor of a speedy entrance to the Grand Lodge on high, where the G.A. of T.U. forever resides, and where, seated at his right hand, he may be pleased to pronounce us upright men and Masons (54:125).

This approval is promised to members of all religions. As we previously noted, the teaching of salvation by personal merit is found not only in the first three degrees of the Blue Lodge, but also in all the higher degrees of the Scottish and York Rites. Time and again, Masonry teaches that a man must be "worthy of life after death" (92:140; see 83:76) and that entrance into the Celestial Lodge is possible if the candidate is willing to give "service and obedience" to Masonry (52:85) and thus live his life regulated by "morality, faith* and justice" (82,II:38).

Blue Lodge ritual makes its mark on those who learn it properly. We have yet to meet a former Mason who disagrees that Masonry teaches salvation by works, or that its teachings are contrary to Christianity. And much authoritative Masonic literature agrees.

---

* The "faith" spoken of comprises faith in the God of one's religion, in Masonry, in the specific masonic deity, or in a combination of these.

Former Masons on Masonry

Former thirty-third-degree Worshipful Master Jim Shaw recalls,

> Never in all my years of dedicated service to Masonry did anyone in the lodge witness to me about the love and saving grace of Jesus. The lodge attended a church once each year as a group. Each time the pastor (who was himself a Mason) would introduce us to the congregation and then exalt the craft, telling them about all our wonderful works. We usually left the church thinking of how wonderful we were and feeling sorry for all those in the church who were not Masons, participating in all our good deeds (20:125).

Eddy Field was a Southern California businessman and member of the Blue Lodge and similar organizations for a quarter-century. He became a thirty-second-degree Mason, Royal Arch Mason, Knight Templar, and Shriner. In addition to being a Lodge officer, he held office in the Cryptic Council, membership in the Eastern Star, Grotto, High 12, Amaranth, and White Shrine of Jerusalem. In "Freemasonry and the Christian," he and his son report,

> After his conversion to Christ, Mr. Field carefully examined the origin and nature of the Lodge and discovered many grave problems with it. He compared the religious teachings of Freemasonry with those of Christianity and found them to be opposite. Therefore, he felt compelled to leave the Lodge....
>
> The Lodge teaches clearly that one may earn admittance into heaven on the basis of works, regardless of religion. This is a false Gospel, which places those who advocate such a doctrine under Paul's imprecation....These facts demonstrate that Christian participation in the Lodge is more than a matter of individual Christian conscience. It is imperative that Christians not participate in this organization....
>
> The soteriology [doctrine of salvation] of Freemasonry is strongly antibiblical, as several of its teachings indicate—teachings

associated with the Lambskin Apron, how to prepare for heaven, the Perfect Ashlar, the Common Gavel, and how to live a worthwhile life. Christian membership in the Lodge is, therefore, impossible to justify in light of scriptural teachings" (166:146, 156-57,141).

Masonic Authorities Speak

Masonic Sovereign Grand Commander Henry Clausen declared that each of the 32 degrees of the Scottish Rite "teach by ceremony and instruction" that the "noblest purposes and duties of man" are to struggle for his own salvation, that each Mason is to overcome and win—"to reach the spiritual and divine within himself"—because "man is...an eternal soul advancing ever nearer and nearer to perfection" (94:156). The eminent Masonic authority Albert Pike taught that "step by step men must advance toward Perfection; and each Masonic Degree is meant to be one of those steps" (26:136).

The *Guide to the Royal Arch Chapter* charges the chaplain of the Order to instruct men to believe that "by refining our morals, strengthening our virtues, and purifying our minds, [this will] *prepare us for admission* into the society of those above whose happiness will be as endless as it is perfect"(45:258, emphasis added). In one Masonic version of the Bible—the Holman Edition—one can find listed under the Masonic Creed the assertion that "character determines destiny" (81:3). Likewise, each Mason is taught that he can climb his way to heaven by his own good deeds:

> As to the modern Masonic symbolism of the ladder, it is, as Brother Mackey has already said, a symbol of progress, such as it is in all the old initiations. Its three principal rounds, representing Faith, Hope, and Charity, present us with the means of advancing from earth to heaven, from death to life—from the mortal to immortality. Hence its foot is placed on the ground floor of the Lodge, which is

typical of the world, and its top rests on the covering of the Lodge, which is symbolic of heaven (96,I:499).

As we see from the above, Masonic authorities everywhere—Coil, Mackey, Clausen, Pike, and others—all teach that men are saved and granted entrance to heaven by their good works. Numerous additional Masonic publications agree. For example, Pennsylvania Grand Chaplain Charles Lacquement writes,

> Freemasonry has been teaching for centuries...the capability of man to reach a higher level of perfection through education and training....The philosophy of Freemasonry is to make man the master of his own destiny, to show him that there also is an immortality on earth brought by his actions; that he can, through his own efforts,...inscribe his name in the "Book of Life" (120:7).

In his *Lexicon of Freemasonry*, Mackey defined the Masonic term *acacian* as "signifying a Mason who by living in strict obedience to obligations and precepts of the fraternity is free from sin" (20:132; see 34:5). In other words, to become a moral person by obedience to Masonic precepts is to be redeemed from sin. Thus, by his initiation and resolve to enter the Masonic life, the Master Mason "has discovered the knowledge of God and His salvation, and been redeemed from the death of sin and the sepulcher of pollution and unrighteousness" (90:44).

Masons believe that their deeds are sufficient to actually merit or deserve God's approval and earn His favor. "Freemasons worship the Creator through acts *deserving* of divine approval" (80:254, emphasis added). They are told, "By...a pure and blameless life,...He [God] will be pleased to pronounce us just and upright Masons" (58:132).

Is Masonic Teaching Sufficient?

Henry Wilson Coil describes how many Masons depend solely on the teachings of the Masonic Lodge to get them into heaven:

> Freemasonry has a religious service to commit the body of a deceased brother to the dust whence it came, and to speed the liberated spirit back to the Great Source of Light. Many Freemasons make this flight with *no other guarantee of a safe landing than their belief in the religion of Freemasonry* (95:512, emphasis added).

From all this, wouldn't you think that you could go to the "Celestial Lodge Above" if you trusted what Masonry taught you, lived a pure life, and engaged in good deeds? Isn't this teaching a person that he can be saved by his own works and personal righteousness? When the Lodge teaches a man that by his good life and by his good deeds God will admit him into heaven, isn't that contrary to Christian teaching? Isn't that "another gospel" (Galatians 1:6-8)? If you are a Christian, what do you think about the fact that all Masons are literally sworn to uphold this Masonic doctrine—and that they even take bloody oaths that impose serious penalties upon themselves if they ever betray it (see question 38)?

Notice the wording of the charge to the third-degree Master Mason:

> My brother,…you are now bound, by duty, honor, and gratitude, to be faithful to your trust; to support the dignity of your character on every occasion; and to enforce, by precept and example, obedience to the tenets of Freemasonry….Your virtue, honor and reputation are concerned in supporting with dignity the character you now bear. Let no motive, therefore, make you swerve from your duty, violate your vows, or betray your trust; but be true and faithful (62:69-70).

Steven Tsoukalas, author of *Masonic Rites and Wrongs*, studied Masonry for almost ten years, in order to discuss it with his father, who was a Mason. About the issue of salvation, he concluded,

> All the evidence from the various Masonic rituals and monitors points to Freemasonry's concern for the removal of estrangement between God and man. The whole ritualistic practice of prayer

offered to T.G.A.O.T.U., the symbolism of darkness characterized by the Hoodwink, the coming of the candidate to light as symbolized by the Volume of the Sacred Law, and the doctrine of the immortality of the soul (in some Grand Lodges the doctrine of a resurrection to a future life) have the sole purpose of removing the estrangement between God and man. In this sense the Masonic Lodge mediates between its candidates and God. Forgiveness of sins is strongly implied in Blue Lodge rituals and in the burial services...of certain Masonic Grand Lodges. The symbolism of the Lambskin Apron, the Common Gavel, the Covering of a Lodge, and the Three Steps allude to a glorious afterlife in the presence of God, implying that one's sins have been forgiven; it is not uncommon to find Masonic magazines stating that brother so-and-so has entered the "Celestial [Lodge above]," or "Grand Lodge, above" (168:86-87).

To reinforce this point, note that the end of the prayer of the Master Mason degree (involving the legend of Hiram Abiff) asks God to "save them with an everlasting salvation" (168: 81). Obviously, Masonry is very concerned with salvation—but regrettably not of the biblical form.

10

DO MANY MASONS DENY THAT MASONRY TEACHES SALVATION BY WORKS?

In a debate on *The John Ankerberg Show,* thirty-second-degree Mason and Christian William Mankin looked straight into the eyes of the audience and told them that Masonry

is not a religion. It offers no system of salvation....Our symbols are related to the development of character, of the relationship of man to man. They are working tools to be used in the building of life. These working tools have been used from time immemorial to build buildings, and all we are saying is that if you as an individual adopt the principles represented [in Masonry]…you will be a better person. Not that you're going to go to heaven (1:2).

An official response to critics of Masonry published by the Masonic Information Center declares plainly,

> Some believe Freemasonry teaches that salvation may be attained by one's good works. *Masonry does not teach any path to salvation.* That is the job of a church, not a fraternity…. Masonry does not teach universalism nor any other doctrine of salvation (165, emphasis added)

In a similar fashion, the Board of General Purposes of the United Grand Lodge of England published a tract titled "Freemasonry and Religion" (102:20). It plainly asserts that Masonry "does *not* claim to lead to salvation by works, by secret knowledge, or by any other means" (102:34 emphasis added).

These statements support the official belief that "Masonry is not a religion," an issue we will examine in our next section. Masons who are familiar with what their Lodge teaches know better. As former Worshipful Master Mason Jack Harris recalls,

> In all the rituals that I taught for eleven years, Masonry did teach how to get to heaven. They taught it with the apron that I wore, by my purity [of] life and conduct. They taught it in the Hiram Abiff legend in the third degree [symbolizing] the immortality of the soul. Through all their writings they say they are teaching the immortality of the soul to the Mason. But the Word of God tells me that the only way to have immortal life is through the Person of Jesus Christ. Never at any Masonic ritual did they point out that Jesus is the way of salvation (13:35).

If Masonry tells Christians or anyone that it is *not* teaching a system of salvation by works, then it is being less than frank with them. A testimony from the terrible days of the Civil War may be sufficient to powerfully illustrate the problem. Steven Merritt was a Christian and Master of the largest lodge in New York. Eventually, he "found the tendency of the whole thing evil,...so I protested and left." In particular, he left Masonry because of his experience with a friend wounded on the battlefield and how it awoke his own conscience:

> One incident helped to open my eyes. I have always preached that there is no other name but Christ by which we can be saved. But again and again I found Masons dying without God and without hope. I was called to the bedside of one member of my lodge who was thought to be dying. He gave me the grip as I sat down by him. He said he was dying and was in great distress for his soul. I tried to have him look to Christ. But he reproached me, saying I had led him astray. I had told him in the lodge, as Master, that a moral life was enough. He said, "You told me then that it was all right if I was an upright man, and obeyed the precepts of the lodge, but I am leaning on a broken reed; and now I am dying without God. I lay this to your charge, Worshipful Master. I leaned on you and now I am dying" (46:55).

Nothing less than this is involved in the issue of Masonry and Christianity: How, precisely does one get to heaven? Is it by Masonry and good works, or by personal faith in Jesus Christ? Stephen Merritt spoke plainly: When "ministers and other good men are in the Lodge, they help to make it a delusion and a snare" (46:55).

THE RELIGION OF MASONRY

Symbolically and spiritually you have been reborn. This started the moment you were prepared to become a Freemason.

—ALLEN E. ROBERTS, *THE CRAFT AND ITS SYMBOLS*

11

DO MASONS INSIST THAT MASONRY IS NOT A RELIGION?

Just as Masonry is less than candid concerning its teachings of salvation by works, it is also less than open about its religious nature. The great majority of Masons will agree with Pennsylvania Grand Chaplain Charles Lacquement: "Freemasonry is not a religion, it is a philosophy" (120:7). Masons will go out of their way to maintain that Masonry is not a religion or a substitute for religion and—in places where Christianity is influential—assert that it helps and supports the Christian Church.

Why is the claim that "Masonry is not a religion" (52:24) found seemingly everywhere in Masonic literature? For instance,

- Masonic authority Silas Shepherd writes, "There is nothing better understood among Masons than that it is not a religion; it is not a religious institution in the sense that it is an instrument for the propagation of religious doctrines" (51,I:138).

- One of the largest apologetic Masonic sites declares, "It is *not* a religion nor does it teach a religious philosophy.... Masons know full well that Freemasonry is no more a religion than is golf, Scouting, or the U.S. Navy League" (167).

- Mason Ed King, founder of the award-winning "Anti-Masonry Points of View" Web site, lists the following things religions do: practice sacerdotal functions, teach theology, ordain clergy, define sin and salvation, perform sacraments, publish or specify a holy book, and describe or define the deity. Then he emphasizes, *"Freemasonry does NONE of these things—but religions DO!"* (194).

As we will see, what proves that Masonry is a religion is the dictionary definition of the word and Masonic belief and practice; nothing else is needed. Further, Ed King's list above is not entirely valid: for example, Masonry does have its own deity that it describes and defines, and a rudimentary theology and creed as well. (Degrees 19 through 30 of the Scottish Rite seek "to explain as clearly and as accurately as possible the nature of Deity and the relationship between Him and mankind"—177:157-58.)

In sum, the reason for the denial is simple. Masonry cannot admit it is a religion because it understands that most men will not leave their own religion to practice *another* religion that actually denies their particular faith. Further, it is central to the nature of Masonry to keep the "higher truths"—the religious truths— from the "unenlightened" members. Albert Pike, for an example, declares that the Blue Lodge degrees are just the outer court of the Temple, not the inner sanctuary, and that the initiate "is intentionally misled by false interpretations. It is not intended that he shall understand them; but it is intended that he shall imagine he understands them. Their true explication is reserved for the Adepts, the Princes of Masonry" (26:818-19).

Here are some similar or additional arguments Masons make when they claim that Masonry is not a religion:

- It lacks the basic elements of religion and has no intention of being a religion in that it has no dogma, theology, or creed.
- It has no desire to enforce an orthodox religion.
- It has no sacraments.
- It does not claim to lead to salvation, either by good works, secret knowledge, or any other means.
- It advocates no sectarian faith or practice.
- It seeks no converts.
- It does not raise money for religious purposes.

None of these claims are true, as we document here and as numerous Masonic critics have previously documented.*

One of the seemingly persuasive arguments made is that Masonry does not fit any standard definition of religion. As the Masonic Service Association of North America concludes, "By *any* definition of religion accepted by our critics, we cannot qualify as a religion" (195). Masonic author Alphonse Cerza quotes the Grand Master of the Grand Lodge in Massachusetts as repeating exactly the same words (73:41).

To the contrary, is there any accepted definition of religion that Masonry does *not* fit? It is absolutely clear that Masonry is a religion. Here is a brief standard definition of religion from *Webster's New World Dictionary*:

> 1: belief in a divine or super human power...to be obeyed and worshipped as the Creator and ruler of the universe;
> 2: [an] expression of...[this] belief in conduct and ritual (106).

---

* From Wagner (16) in the early twentieth century to Tsoukalas (168) in the early twenty-first century.

We will proceed to illustrate that Masons cannot logically deny that Freemasonry fits this definition of religion.

12

BY REQUIRING ITS MEMBERS TO BELIEVE IN A SUPREME BEING, DOES MASONRY FIT WEBSTER'S DEFINITION OF A RELIGION?

First, Masons freely acknowledge that Masonry *requires* belief in a Supreme Being. In fact, with the exception of one country out of more than 100 (France), atheists are not permitted Lodge membership. The greatest and most central doctrine in Masonry is belief in the existence of God. It is so fundamental that without it there is simply no Masonry (51,I:12-13). The Tennessee monitor (as do other monitors) reveals that in the very first degree, the Entered Apprentice degree, the candidate is required to pledge he believes in God:

THE CANDIDATE'S ASSENT IS REQUIRED TO THE FOLLOWING DECLARATIONS:

Do you seriously declare upon your honor, that you believe in a Supreme Being to whom all men are accountable?

Answer. I do (65:6).

Not only is each Mason required to swear he believes in God, but the Lodge is required to dedicate each candidate in prayer to the "Almighty Father of the Universe." Each man who enters the Lodge is intentionally dedicated to God's service, and it is specifically stated in the Masonic ritual that it will be through "the secrets of our art" that God will be revealed and honored. Here is the actual prayer that is said in every lodge for candidates being initiated into the Entered Apprentice degree:

Vouchsafe Thine aid, Almighty Father of the Universe, to this our present convention; and grant that this candidate for Freemasonry may dedicate and devote his life to Thy service, and become a true and faithful brother among us. Endue him with a competency of Thy divine wisdom, that by the secrets of our art he may better be enabled to display the beauties of godliness to the honor of Thy holy name. Amen.

Response: So mote [may] it be (69:13).

From this it can be seen that Masonry does fulfill the first requirement of Webster's definition of religion—namely, that the candidate and each person in the Lodge must believe in a Supreme Being.

13

BY REQUIRING ITS MEMBERS TO OBEY GOD, DOES MASONRY FIT WEBSTER'S DEFINITION OF A RELIGION?

The entire ritualistic system of Masonry is based upon obedience to God. In its many degrees, Masonry requires each candidate to swear numerous oaths to God; prayers are set forth for the candidate to ask God for His divine power to enable the candidate to live for Him as a Mason and to serve or obey Him. The individual Mason must swear that he will keep his promises to God (see question 38). The Masonic manual for the second (Fellow Craft) degree sets forth the following prayer to be said over the candidate during this ceremony:

> Grant, O Father Almighty, to this Candidate for more light, the continuance of Thy divine favor, that he may improve in Freemasonry, and in the knowledge of Thy Word and all liberal art and science. Keep him a faithful brother among us; truly serving Thee all the days of his life (64:36).

The third (Master Mason) degree closes with a prayer asking God to give the member a greater awareness of the obligations that the Masons are placed under to love and obey God (54:128). Whether it be the first, second, third, or other Masonic degree, each candidate is instructed that he is to obey God. The Arkansas *Masonic Monitor* offers this closing prayer for the Entered Apprentice degree: "Supreme Architect of the Universe,…make us sensible of our obligations to serve Thee, and may all our actions tend to Thy glory and our advancement in knowledge and virtue" (62:9).

So again, the evidence shows that Masons who practice and follow their ritual ceremonies are fulfilling Webster's next requirement of religion, obedience to God. And here it must be asked, which God does the Mason swear his obedience to? Many American Masons assume that it is the biblical God they are praying to and swearing oaths to. But as we will show later (see section V), when the Mason obeys and serves the God of the Lodge, he is not obeying the God of the Bible.

14

BY REQUIRING ITS MEMBERS TO WORSHIP GOD AS THE CREATOR AND RULER OF THE UNIVERSE, DOES MASONRY FIT WEBSTER'S DEFINITION OF A RELIGION?

Masonry is full of worship to God as the creator and ruler of the universe. In Clausen's words, "Freemasons worship the Creator" (80:254). Pike's *Liturgy of the Scottish Rite* refers to God as "the Supreme, Self-existent, Eternal,…Merciful Creator and Preserver of the Universe" (93:162, as cited in 168:143).

Webster's dictionary defines "worship" as "a prayer...or other rite showing reverence or devotion for a deity"—for God, that is (108). Do Masons have rites that instruct them how to show reverence and give devotion to God? Masonry has nearly 40 degrees of ritual instructing Masons how to live a good life before God and how to please Him. According to Webster, in actuality, Masons are worshiping every time they practice the ceremonies of the Lodge. Masonic authority Allen E. Roberts writes,

Masons walk in his [God's] presence continually....[In ritual, the candles] formed a triangle about the altar at which you knelt in reverence. They symbolized the presence of Deity....The Masonic altar can be said to be one of sacrifice....You have taken the obligations [to God] that have sacrificed your self-interest forevermore" (79:57,64).

The *Standard Masonic Monitor* commands,

Let no man enter any great or important undertaking without first invoking the aid of Deity....The trust of a Mason is in God (54:17).

Claudy agrees that this is worship:

Freemasonry's lodges are erected to God....Symbolically, to "erect to God" means to construct something in honor, in worship, in reverence to and for him. Hardly is the initiate within the West Gate before he is impressed that Freemasonry worships God (55:23).

Do all of the rites in Masonry show reverence and devotion to a deity? There is no doubt of it. In fact, every Mason, by his good works and worship of the Masonic deity, is said to be actually erecting a divine temple in his heart that the deity himself will inhabit. Masonic monitors give the following instruction to initiates of the first degree:

My brother,...this ceremony has the following significance: As the operative Mason [the medieval stonemason] has a corner stone usually placed in the northeast corner, upon which to erect his temporal building, so should the speculative Mason [modern Mason] have a corner stone upon which to erect his spiritual temple. This corner stone is his initiatory instruction. You have this night commenced the great task, which in your future Masonic life should never be discontinued, that of *erecting in your heart a temple of the indwelling of God* (65:13, emphasis added).

Masonry unquestionably fulfills this characteristic of religion, in that it worships God as the creator and ruler of the universe.

How Should a Christian Mason Respond to This?

Has Masonry set itself up as a replacement for the religious activity of the church? In Scripture, God tells us that Jesus Christ is the cornerstone and foundation of the believer's spiritual life, not the ideas of the Lodge. Christ is the one by whom the temple of God is being built inside of us. It is being built through individual Christians who confess faith in Christ. The cornerstone and foundation of the believer's life is Jesus Christ. The Bible contradicts what Masonry teaches with these words:

> You are no longer foreigners and aliens, but fellow citizens with God's people and members of God's household, built on the foundation of the apostles and prophets, with Christ Jesus himself as the chief cornerstone. In him the whole building is joined together and rises to become a holy temple in the Lord (Ephesians 2:19-21 NIV).

> You..., like living stones, are being built into a spiritual house to be a holy priesthood, offering spiritual sacrifices acceptable to God through Jesus Christ (1 Peter 2:5 NIV).

> I lay "a stone in Zion, a chosen and precious cornerstone, and the one who trusts in him will never be put to shame." Now to you who believe, this stone is precious. But to those who do not believe, "The stone the builders rejected has become the capstone (1 Peter 2:6-7 NIV).

15

BY REQUIRING ITS MEMBERS TO EXPRESS BELIEF IN GOD IN CONDUCT AND RITUAL, DOES MASONRY FIT WEBSTER'S DEFINITION OF A RELIGION?

In the higher degrees of the York and Scottish rites, we find much additional evidence that Masonry is, in fact, a religion. The higher rites are full of instruction about God, and how to worship God, about religious ritual and symbol, and so on. For example, the seventeenth degree of the Scottish rite tells the candidate "that

Masonry is of divine origin" and that alleged Masonic forerunners "took an oath to spend the last drop of their blood to establish the true religion of the most high God" (59,I:453). Joseph Fort Newton wrote,

> Everything in Masonry has reference to God, implies God, speaks of God, points and leads to God. Not a degree, not a symbol, not an obligation, not a lecture, not a charge but finds its meaning and derives its beauty from God the Great Architect, in whose temple all Masons are workmen (18:58-59).

It should be clear that Freemasonry fits Webster's definition of religion in every point. Freemasonry teaches its members that they must swear to belief in God. Every degree in Masonry offers prayers to God. Oaths are regularly taken in the name of God. Masons understand that their first duty is to obey God. Everything in Masonry is said to be given in worship to God. All Masonic rites offer religious forms and ceremonies. Masons are building God's own temple through their good works. A Mason should never undertake any significant task without invoking the blessing of God, and so on.

Further, as we documented elsewhere, from the rituals, and beliefs of Masonry, we can see that Masonry 1) has its own religious creed, 2) has its own distinct religious doctrinal statement like a church, 3) has its own unique theology, and 4) uses religious symbols like those found in a church (135:7-25). Just because Masonry chooses not to be identified as a religion does not change matters. In all the world, perhaps no one who has seriously studied Masonry will deny that Masonry is a religion except Masons themselves.

There Can Be No Doubt

In *The Encyclopedia of Philosophy,* William Alston cites the following characteristics of religion:

- A belief in supernatural beings (God or gods)

- A distinction between sacred and profane objects
- Ritual acts that are focused upon such sacred objects
- A moral code that has supernatural sanction
- Religious feelings which are aroused by sacred objects or ritual and connected in idea with God or gods
- Prayer
- A particular worldview which encompasses the individual's place within the world
- The more or less total organization of one's life based on such a worldview
- A social group that is bound together by the above traits (208)

We have read or examined more than 100 books by Masons about Masonry, and it is plain that Masonry contains the above characteristics.* After almost ten years of research in Masonry, Steven Tsoukalas concluded likewise: Masonry's "Blue Lodge ritual fulfills the essential characteristics of a religion" (168:37). Indeed, Masonry is proven a religion not only by its ritual, but by its declarations, history, symbols (168), worldview, burial services (168:100-118)—and even its own authorities.

Masonry is unquestionably a religion, and Masons are participating in a religion, whether or not they know it.

16

Do Many Leading Masons Admit that Masonry Is a Religion?

Many of the most respected Masonic authorities who have written on this issue have admitted that Masonry is a religion or

---

* While space does not permit the exposition of these nine specific characteristics item by item, they are documented in our earlier books and point by point in Steven Tsoukalas' *Masonic Rites and Wrongs*, which also offers possibly the best critique of Masonic ritual per se (168:24-37).

is religious. Henry Wilson Coil's *A Comprehensive View of Freemasonry* plainly asserts, "Religion is espoused by the Masonic ritual and required of the candidate" (36:186). In fact, his entire discussion of the issue (some 15,000 words) in *Coil's Masonic Encyclopedia* proves beyond doubt that Masonry is a religion. And he clearly affirms that "Freemasonry is undoubtedly religion" (95:158) and speaks of Freemasons' "belief in the religion of Freemasonry" (95:512 emphasis added).

Mackey's *Encyclopedia of Freemasonry* declares that "the *religion* of Masonry is cosmopolitan, universal" (173: 301, emphasis added). Elsewhere, Mackey states that

> Freemasonry may rightfully claim to be called a religious institution....The tendency of all true Freemasonry is toward religion....Look at its ancient landmarks [doctrines], its sublime ceremonies, its profound symbols and allegories—all inculcating religious doctrine, commanding religious observance, and teaching religious truth, and *who can deny that it is eminently a religious Institution?*....We open and close our Lodges with prayer; we invoke the blessing of the Most High upon all our labors; we demand of our neophytes a profession of trusting belief in the existence and the superintending care of God;....it is impossible that a Freemason can be "true and trusty" to his Order unless he is a respecter of religion and an observer of religious principle (96,II:847, emphasis added).

In the *Liturgy of the Scottish Rite,* Albert Pike declares, "Every Masonic Lodge is a temple of religion; and its teachings are instruction in religion." He further explains that the Mason's "reward is the knowledge of the True God" and that "Masonry is a worship....It is the *universal, eternal, immutable religion,* such as God planted it in the heart of universal humanity"(93:167,198-99, emphasis added). Joseph Fort Newton wrote an entire book titled *The Religion of Masonry* (18). In his *Introduction to Freemasonry,* Carl Claudy teaches that "God is the very warp and woof of

Freemasonry....Take God out of Freemasonry and there is, literally, nothing left" (60,II:109).

Many scholars also declare Masonry a religion. Dr. Shildes Johnson holds three doctorates in religion or fields relating to religion. In *Is Masonry a Religion?* he concludes, "A comparison of the moral, allegorical, and symbolic teachings of Freemasonry with these definitions of a religion reveals that the lodge is a theistic, non-Christian, man-centered, and universal religion" (15:21). Additional sources could be listed: numerous secular researchers (for example, 12:310; 6:302); Christian writers (for example, 4:15-20); dozens of independent investigations by church committees (102; 103; 104; 166; see 11:6-7) and other Masonic authors (for example, 51,I:153; 52:121; 57:89-90). All conclude that Masonry is a religion.

17

DOES MASONRY TEACH THAT IT IS THE ONE TRUE RELIGION ON EARTH?

Freemasonry...is the ground which underlies all religions, all churches, all creeds, all sects (209).

—"THE CRAFT'S ATTITUDE TO POLITICS AND RELIGION," GRAND LODGE OF BRITISH COLUMBIA AND YUKON WEB SITE

Masonry teaches that non-Masons are living in spiritual darkness and that only the Lodge leads men into spiritual light. In the first degree, the candidate is told he "has long been in darkness, and now seeks to be brought to light" (58:29). Mackey refers to the candidate in these words:

> There he stands without [outside] our portals, on the threshold of his new Masonic life, in darkness, helplessness and ignorance. Having been wandering amid the errors and covered over with the

pollutions of the outer and profane world, he comes inquiringly to our door, seeking the new birth, and asking a withdrawal of the veil which conceals divine truth from his uninitiated sight (105:20).

The twenty-eighth degree teaches that

> the first degree represents man, when he had sunken from his original lofty estate....He is emphatically a profane, enveloped in darkness, poor and destitute of spiritual knowledge, and emblematically naked. The material darkness which is produced by the bandage over his eyes, is an emblem of the darkness of his soul (59,II: 221-22).

In the thirtieth degree it is finally declared to the initiate in unmistakable terms that his earlier religious beliefs are merely harmful superstitions and that the claim of religious compatibility was only a ruse to get him on course in Masonry. Indeed, at this point Masonry's true colors are now revealed:

> In all the preceding degrees you must have observed that the object of Scotch Masonry is to *overthrow all kinds of superstition*, and that by admitting in her bosom on the terms of the strictest equality, the members of all religions, of all creeds and of all countries, without any distinction whatever, she has, and indeed can have, but one single object and that is to restore to the Grand Architect of the Universe; to the common father of the human race, those who are *lost in the maze of impostures, invented for the sole purpose of enslaving them*. The Knights Kadosh recognize no particular religion, and for that reason we demand of you nothing more than to worship God. And whatever may be the religious forms imposed upon you by superstition at a period of your life when you were incapable of discerning truth from falsehood, we do not even require you to relinquish them. Time and study alone can enlighten you. But remember that you will never be a true mason unless you *repudiate forever all superstitions and prejudices* (59,II: 263-64, emphasis added).

From this it can be seen that Masonry teaches that of all the faiths in the world, it alone is the true faith and ultimately all other religions are false superstitions. With such a belief, Masonry can hardly claim that it "respects all religions" or that it seeks to unite all religions into a common brotherhood. The only way Masonry really seeks to unite all men is to have them *abandon* their particular religious beliefs.

As Joseph Fort Newton points out, "Masonry seeks to free men from a limiting conception of religion, and thus to remove one of the chief causes of sectarianism." Newton hopes that as Masonry expands around the world, "all religious dogmas will cease to be." All individual creeds and doctrines will be done away with, and what remains will be what is termed "the one eternal religion— the Fatherhood of God, the brotherhood of man, the moral law, the golden rule, and the hope of a life everlasting!" (77:243,246-47).

Masonry truly believes itself to be a "Holy Empire," whose mission is "to dispel darkness." Thus, it is the mission and "duty of its initiates to diffuse among men its ideals, without which error, superstition and spiritual subjugation *must be eternal*" (52:123, emphasis added). Thirty-third-degree Mason Manly P. Hall says that the Mason, because he is "freed of limitation of creed and sect, stands as master of all faiths" (35:13). This is also the reason Albert Pike argued that "humanity has never really had but one religion and one worship" (26:102). As we noted in question 15, the seventeenth degree of the Scottish rite tells the candidate that "Masonry is of divine origin" and that Masonic forerunners "took an oath to spend the last drop of their blood to establish the *true religion* of the most high God" (59,I:453, emphasis added).

Indeed, in the thirtieth degree of the Scottish Rite, the candidate is taught that "Jehovah" (whom it equates with the Great Architect of the Universe) created Masonry:

> When the spirit of God moved upon the face of the waters;
> when the Great Jehovah ordained the creation of the

world; when the first Sun rose to greet with its beams, the new morning and the august command was uttered: "Let there be light," the lips of deity breathed Masonry into existence and it must live forevermore; for truth is eternal, and the principles of truth are the foundation of Masonry (59,II:290).

Differentiating the god of Masonry from the god of other faiths, Albert Mackey could confidently say, "Freemasons have always been worshippers of the one true God" (16:290). Thus, once Masons are aware that Masonry is the one true religion, they cannot help but "strip from all religions their orthodox tenets, legends, allegories and dogmas" (94:157).

A Superior Religion?

The following statements by respected Masonic authors and leaders demonstrate conclusively that Masonry presents itself as a religion superior to other faiths.

Former Freemason Edmond Ronayne has stated, "Freemasonry claims to be the only true religion now in the world." He cites McClenachan's *Book of the Ancient and Accepted Scottish Rite* as promising, "Masonry at last shall conquer, and its altar be the world" (31:111-12). Albert Pike taught that Masonry

> is the universal, eternal, immutable religion, such as God planted it in the heart of universal humanity....
>
> Masonry teaches, and has preserved in their purity, the cardinal tenets of the old primitive [universal] faith, which underlie and are the foundation of all religions. All that ever existed have had a basis of truth; and all have overlaid that truth with errors. [For example,] the primitive truths taught by the Redeemer [Jesus] were sooner corrupted and intermingled and alloyed with fictions than when taught to the first of our race. Masonry is thus the universal morality which is suitable to the inhabitants of every clime, to the man of every creed (26:161,219).

For Masons, "in all ages, the golden thread of Truth have gleamed in the woof of Error," and only the initiate in the Lodge with his "True Masonic Light" can see the golden threads and "read them aright" (51,V:52). In other words, only Masonry knows and can point out the true thread of truth within the massive error of another religion. Only Masonry has retained the core truth God intended for humanity in its entirety. In this regard, Masonic authors have believed and taught the following:

> There is under all creeds one universal religion (89:99).

> This one true religion…is the very soul of Masonry (77:258).

> The true disciple of ancient Masonry has given up forever the worship of personalities….As a Mason his religion must be universal: Christ, Buddha or Mohammed, the names mean little, for he recognizes only the Light and not the bearer (35:64-65).

> It is true that Masonry is not a religion, but it is Religion….religions are many; Religion is one….It brings together men of all creeds in behalf of those truths which are greater than all sects, deeper than all doctrines (77:243).

> Scarcely a Masonic discourse is pronounced or a Masonic lesson read, by the highest officer or the humblest lecturer, that does not earnestly teach this one true religion which is the very soul of Masonry, its basis and apex, its light and power. Upon that faith it rests; and in that faith it lives and labors; and by that faith it will conquer at last (77:258).

From all this we can see that the Masonic claim to tolerance and respect for other religions is a charade. Masonry respects the beliefs of other religions only when those religions agree with its own; the other beliefs it discards as so much chaff. Masonry says it tolerates and respects the religious beliefs of others, but it really intends to change and replace them. What other conclusion is possible if Masonry hopes to rid the world of all its "unenlightened" dogmas and other "superstitious beliefs" in order to generate a supposed universal brotherhood?

Extensive reading in Masonic literature makes clear that Masonry is a substitute religion, however emphatically it may attempt to deny this. The more one reads in Masonry, the more obvious and undeniable it becomes that Masonry believes and claims that it alone is the one true religion (95:512; 76:18; 51,V:35; 77:62-63,275). To say the least, Christian Masons who realize that the goal of Masonry is to replace Christianity with its own religion should discontinue their support (205).

THE BIBLE OF MASONRY

18

IS THE HOLY BIBLE REALLY THE "GREAT LIGHT IN MASONRY" AND THE RULE AND GUIDE FOR MASONIC FAITH AND PRACTICE?

Just as Masonry claims that it does not teach a system of salvation (but does), and that it is not a religion (but is), Masonry also claims that it honors the Bible as God's Word—but it doesn't. First, let us examine what Masonry says. The *Standard Masonic Monitor* maintains that the Bible is "the Great Light in Masonry" and even advises Masons to study it diligently:

> I particularly direct your attention to the Great Light in Masonry, the Holy Bible. Howsoever men differ in creed or theology, all good men are agreed that within the covers of the Holy Bible are found those principles of morality which lay the foundation upon which to build a righteous life. Freemasonry therefore opens this Book on its altars, with the command to each of its votaries that he diligently study therein to learn the way to everlasting life (54:21).

Another standard source reads, "No Mason needs to be told what a great place the Bible has in the Masonry of our day....

While we honor every Book of Faith...with us the Bible is supreme....Its truth is inwrought in the fiber of our being" (51,IV:215-218).

The Arkansas *Masonic Monitor* declares the following: "The three great lights in Masonry are the Holy Bible, Square and Compass, and are thus explained: the Holy Bible is given us as the rule and guide for our faith and practice" (62:15).

Masonry teaches that the All-Seeing Eye (God) and the Lambskin (the apron) are meant to show the Mason that his purity of life and conduct will earn him his right to be in God's heaven. However, nowhere is the doctrine of salvation by works taught in the Bible (see question 8). This alone shows that Masons do not accept the Bible as their "rule of faith and practice."

19

WHAT DOES THE BIBLE ACTUALLY SYMBOLIZE IN MASONRY?

In the Holman Temple Illustrated Edition of the Holy Bible—a Masonic edition—Joseph Fort Newton points out the following in his article "The Bible and Masonry":

> The Bible, so rich in symbolism, is itself a symbol....It is a sovereign symbol of the Book of Faith, the will of God as man has learned it in the midst of the years—that perpetual revelation of himself which God is making to mankind in every land in every age. Thus, by the very honor which Masonry pays to the Bible, it teaches us to revere every book of faith...joining hands with the man of Islam as he takes oath on the Koran, and with the Hindu as he makes covenant with God upon the book that he loves best. For Masonry knows what so many forget, that religions are many, but Religion is one—perhaps we may say one thing....Therefore it invites to its altar men of all faiths knowing that, if they use different names for "the Nameless

One of a hundred names," they are yet praying to the one God and Father of all; knowing, also, that while they read different volumes, they are in fact reading the same vast Book of the Faith of Man (81:3-4).

From this quote we can see that the Bible is not a "rule and guide for faith and practice," but just a symbol. We all know what a symbol is. The American flag is a symbol of freedom. The flag itself is not freedom; it is a piece of brightly colored cloth that symbolizes freedom. In the same way, Masonry teaches that the Bible itself is not God's Word, but is a book that symbolizes God's Word—that is, His true revelations dimly seen in all religions, most clearly revealed in Masonry. This is why the Bible is officially designated as a piece of "lodge furniture." Furniture may be important in a house, but it is not central. The flag is cloth, the Bible is furniture. They are only important because they represent or symbolize something else.

The "Core Truths"

The Bible is supposed to symbolize the "will of God" as defined by Masonry. The "will of God"—which supposedly the Bible and the Scriptures of all faiths point to—turns out to be Masonic doctrine. Masonic truth is the highest truth and revelation of Masonry's deity.

In the quotation above, Newton makes reference to the revelation of God in every religion. Earlier we saw that Masonry believes that its *own* doctrines constitute the "core truths" of all religions. That is why Newton says that "religions are many but Religion [that is, the truth found in Masonry] is one." Included here is the idea that the universal Masonic doctrines have been overlaid with much error by different individual religions.* Thus, Masonry will admit that in all the different scriptures of the world the "revelation of God" can be found in varying degrees, but they understand that it is most fully revealed in Masonry. In this manner they

---

* We expanded on this theme in *The Secret Teachings of the Masonic Lodge* (Moody Press, 1990).

can "accept" all people's scriptures, yet hold that they are but dim reflections, or symbolic teachings, of the greater truth revealed in Masonry.

With this in mind, it should not be surprising to learn that Masons in Utah have the Book of Mormon placed upon the Masonic altar, not the Bible. In India, Masons place the Vedas or Upanishads on their Masonic altar. Masons in Muslim lands place the Koran on their altar. These books are not to be followed literally as truth, but are only to be honored as symbols of Masonic truth.

Why Does Masonry Value the Bible?

What value is the Bible to the Lodge if it only symbolizes truth that must be discovered elsewhere? Albert Pike explains:

> The Bible is an indispensable part of the furniture of a Christian Lodge, *only because* it is the sacred book of the Christian religion. The Hebrew Pentateuch in a Hebrew Lodge, and the Koran in a Mohammedan one, belong on the Altar; and one of these, and the Square and Compass, properly understood, are the Great Lights by which a Mason must walk and work.

> The obligation of the candidate is always to be taken on the sacred book or books of his religion, *that he may deem it more solemn and binding;* and therefore it was that you were asked of what religion you were. *We have no other concern with your religious creed* (26:11, emphasis added).

What does this mean? It means that the real purpose Masonry has for recognizing the scriptures of all faiths is to get men to swear allegiance to *Masonry* on the authority of the scriptures they hold dear. But in doing so, Masonry profanes each faith's holy "symbol." It does this by having men swear upon their sacred scriptures to obey Masonic religious beliefs that deny or distort that which their sacred scriptures really teach.

This leads us to a startling conclusion: Christians (and those of other faiths) have been misled. Masonry has used the Christian's respect for the Bible only to get him to swear allegiance to Masonry. Obviously, Masonry cannot ask a Christian to swear allegiance to Masonry on the Koran or the Upanishads when he does not believe these are the Word of God. But a Christian does believe this of the Bible—and so Masonry asks him to swear upon it. And Masonry practices and believes the same in regards to other faiths and their respective holy books.

Put simply, Masonry does not have much respect for the actual theological content of any holy book—as Pike said, "We have no other concern for your religious creed." So Masonry cares little for the Bible itself—it is more concerned with how the Bible can be used to secure the allegiance of members to Masonic beliefs. In fact, Masonry has never intended that Christians should keep and follow their Scriptures, for to do so would be to oppose the distinctive teachings of Masonry. Anyone who accepts the Bible as his rule of faith and practice would be forced to quit the Lodge.

20

WHAT ARE SIX DISTINCT TEACHINGS OF MASONRY ABOUT THE BIBLE?

From the authorities of Masonry, we learn that the Lodge has at least six distinct teachings about the Bible:

1. *The Bible is a piece of Lodge furniture, a great symbolic "light" upon which the candidate obligates himself to Masonry.*

   Mackey's Revised Encyclopedia of Freemasonry teaches, "In the American system, the Bible is both a piece of furniture and a great light" (96,I:133; 51,I:132).

2. *The Bible is only a symbol of the will of God.*

Masonry teaches that the actual contents of the Bible are not the Word of God. In *Coil's Masonic Encyclopedia* we read, "The prevailing Masonic opinion is that the Bible is only a symbol of Divine Will, Law, or Revelation, and *not that its contents are Divine Law, inspired, or revealed*. So far, no responsible authority has held that a Freemason must believe the Bible or any part of it" (95:520, emphasis added).

Masonic authority Silas H. Shepherd notes, "When our rituals and Monitors tell us the Bible is one of the Great Lights of Masonry and that as such it is the rule and guide to our faith, *it can only be speaking symbolically*, as it certainly is when speaking of the other two Great Lights, the square and the compass" (51,I:129-130, emphasis added).

3. *The Scriptures of other faiths are equally valid for the Mason.*

Mackey's Revised Encyclopedia of Freemasonry explains this: "The Bible is used among Freemasons as a symbol of the will of God, however it may be expressed. Therefore, whatever to any people expresses that will [of God] may be used as a substitute for the Bible in a Masonic Lodge....Whether it be the Gospels to the Christian, the Pentateuch to the Israelite, the Koran to the Musselman [Muslim] or the Vedas to the Brahman [Hindu], it everywhere Masonically conveys the same idea—that of the symbolism of the Divine Will revealed to man" (96,I:133).

4. *The Bible is only part of the "revelation" of God.*

We saw earlier that Joseph Fort Newton referred to "that perpetual revelation of Himself which God is making to mankind in every land in every age. Thus, by the very honor which Masonry pays to the Bible, it teaches us to revere every book of faith" (81:3). In other words, the

Bible is only part of God's revelation to man. The Mason includes all the other Scriptures of the world's major religions as equally valid but equally dim reflections of Masonic truths.

5. *The Bible is not the literal Word of God and is not to be literally obeyed.*

   Masonic scholar Oliver Street teaches, "The Bible is not displayed on our altars now and never has been for the reason that Masons are required to believe its teachings. We know that there is a very large element of the Craft the world over who do not believe the teachings of the New Testament....Hence, unless we are perpetrating a grim mockery, we do not employ the Bible as a profession that we as a Society accept all its teachings and doctrines" (51,I:129; see 95:520).

6. *Masonic doctrine itself is the true (literal) word of God.*

   If Masonry is taught to be the true religion of God (see question 17), and if the scriptures of all faiths are but dim reflections of Masonic truth, and if the "true" teachings inside each religion are the teachings of Masonry, then the logical conclusion is that Masonic doctrine is the true word of God that is to be literally obeyed. Martin Wagner, an early authority on Masonry, observes that "Freemasons take it for granted and as proved that the mystical interpretation of the scriptures according to Kabbalistic principles and methods, is the correct one. The eminent Masons all contend that there is a veil upon the scriptures, which when removed, leaves them clearly in accord with Masonic teachings and in essential harmony with other sacred books" (16:335-336; see 16:341-42).

   Clearly then, Masonry is the only divine truth that is to be literally obeyed.

Other Masonic Teachings About the Bible

In the higher degrees of Masonry, we find additional non-Christian teachings concerning the Bible. For example, it is taught that Christians cannot properly interpret it. In the twenty-eighth degree of the Scottish Rite, Albert Pike declares, "The Hebrew books [of the Bible] were written in Symbols unintelligible to the Profane [that is, the ignorant or the non-Mason]" (26:744-45). In other words, only enlightened Masons can "properly interpret the Bible." Martin Wagner comments,

> Charles Sotheran [a late-nineteenth-century Masonic leader] speaks of the Bible as a pseudo-revelation....Many Masonic writers ridicule the Christian doctrine that the Bible is a supernatural revelation from God. They say it is a book written for the vulgar, by the ancient priests, and that they concealed under its exoteric [outer or normal] language, the secret doctrine, which is the true Freemasonry (16:285).

The Masonic view of the Bible is made especially evident in *Chase's Digest of Masonic Law,* in which the author asserts,

> To require that a candidate profess a belief in the divine authority of the Bible is a serious innovation in the very body of Masonry. The Jews, the Chinese, the Turks, each reject either the Old or the New Testament, or both, and yet we see no good reason why they should not be made Masons. In fact, *Blue Lodge Masonry has nothing whatever to do with the Bible.* It is not founded on the Bible. If it were, *it would not be Masonry* (pp. 207-8 as cited in 19:29, emphasis added).

In conclusion, virtually all Masonic authorities "establish three things: 1) that the Bible is only a symbol, 2) that a Mason is not required to believe the Bible's teachings, and 3) that some other book may be substituted for the Bible" (51,I:132). This is why leading Masonic authority Rollin Blackmer observes that the Bible "is almost never read in the lodge. In thirty years of almost constant attendance at lodge in many jurisdictions, the writer has never heard the Bible read in the lodge, though portions of Scriptures are occasionally quoted in the ritualistic work" (50:22).

21

WHAT DID JESUS AND THE WRITERS
OF THE SCRIPTURES TEACH ABOUT THE BIBLE?

Masonic views are in direct conflict with what the Bible claims for itself:

> All Scripture is inspired by God and profitable for teaching, for reproof, for correction, for training in righteousness; so that the man of God may be adequate, equipped for every good work (2 Timothy 3:16-17).

> No prophecy of Scripture is a matter of one's own interpretation, for no prophecy was ever made by an act of human will, but men moved by the Holy Spirit spoke from God (2 Peter 1:20-21).

> Every word of God is tested; He is a shield to those who take refuge in Him. Do not add to His words, or He will reprove you, and you will be proved a liar (Proverbs 30:5-6).

The teachings of Jesus concerning the Bible are also quite opposite those of Masonry, for example:

> The Scripture cannot be broken (John 10:35).

> Sanctify them in the truth; Your word is truth (John 17:17).

> It is written, "Man shall not live on bread alone, but on every word that proceeds out of the mouth of God" (Matthew 4:4).

> The words which You gave Me I have given to them (John 17:8).

> Heaven and earth will pass away, but My words will not pass away (Matthew 24:35).

> He who rejects Me and does not receive My sayings, has one who judges him; the word I spoke is what will judge him at the last day.

For I did not speak on My own initiative, but the Father Himself who sent Me has given Me commandment as to what to say and what to speak....The things I speak, I speak just as the Father has told Me (John 12:48-50).

Because of the Masonic approach to the Bible, Jesus' teachings about its authority are not appreciated in the Lodge. Rather, the Bible is misquoted or misinterpreted in Masonic rituals and writings to teach the truths of Masonry (for example, 41:45; 82,II:52; 19:43; 58:171-76,181). Most informed Masons believe it is a mistake to interpret the Bible literally because the Bible would flatly contradict what Masonry is teaching. Thus, the Bible should be interpreted allegorically, symbolically, or mystically (26:224,715, 741,744,818; 20:128-29; 99a:15; 103:5).

22

CAN CHRISTIAN MASONS BELIEVE BOTH THE BIBLE AND MASONIC TEACHINGS ABOUT THE BIBLE?

There are certainly hundreds of thousands of Masons who are also Christians. But how can a Christian Mason who claims to believe that the Bible is the literal Word of God then proceed to promote an organization that denies what the Bible teaches about itself and salvation? For instance, Christians know that the Bible is not simply to be read as a symbol or allegory (see the previous question)—or to be misquoted, misinterpreted, and ignored. The Bible is to be obeyed as the literal, inerrant Word of God. Scripture emphasizes this repeatedly. What good does it do to talk about the Bible as the "Great Light" of Masonry if a person never turns on the switch?

Or when Masonry tells a man that "by the secrets of our art" he will be better able to glorify God, is it true for the Christian? The words of the monitor read, "I *assure you* there is nothing therein [in Masonry] that is incompatible with your civil or religious duties, or with those higher and nobler duties which you owe to God, your country, your neighbor, your family, or yourself. With this assurance, do you still desire to proceed?" (65:9, emphasis added). Is this true? As a Christian Mason, didn't you swear, "I should never engage in any undertaking on which I could not invoke the blessing of deity" (65:16)? How can a Christian possibly invoke the blessing of God upon the mistaken teachings stated above?

The charge to a Master Mason in the monitor reads, "The great principles of moral truth and moral government which are unfolded in this and the preceding degrees originated in the Divine Mind" (65:102). As a Christian, do you really think that such teachings on salvation and the Bible originated in God's mind?

Masons at the end of their oaths will kiss the Bible. They will not read it, nor will they obey it, but they will kiss it and swear by it in their oaths—even in the more pagan oaths of the higher degrees (168; 17). As a Christian Mason, does this not concern you?

The God of Masonry

23

Does Masonry Teach that Masons of Contrary Religious Persuasions Actually Worship the Same Deity?

*The man who denies God, and the man
who defines him, with a pretended infallibility,
are equally fanatical [and in] error (99a:16).*

—Legenda 32, part 1

At one level, Masonry accepts that men may worship the deity of their choice. This is the basis for their concept of human brotherhood—to allegedly unite men in fellowship and service to God, but without any discussion as to the particular nature of God that would cause division among them.*

At the basic level, Masons may believe in whatever God they wish to—Jehovah of the Bible, Krishna of the Bhagavad Gita, Brahman of the Hindus, Allah of Islam, various Buddhist deities, and so on—they just can't discuss Him (or It or Them) in the Lodge.

---

* See appendix A for more discussion on why Masonic brotherhood is a logical impossibility; see also 172:192-198. Since all religions claim absolute truth but conflict with each other, having different Gods and contrary beliefs, Masonry, which also claims exclusive, absolute truth, is just another competing religion with its own God—hardly a special unifying force for universal brotherhood.

But remember, there are different levels of Masonic enlighten-ment. Thus, at a higher level Masonry teaches that its God is the *one true God* and that all specific theological conceptions of God in other religions are flawed and fall short of the majesty of this one true God. As Pike's *Liturgy of the Scottish Rite* declares,

> The cherished dogmas of each of us are not, as we fondly suppose, the pure truth of God; but simply our own *special form of error,* our *guesses* at truth....Our little systems have their day, and cease to be; they are but broken lights of God; and he is more than they (93:201-202 as cited in 168:146-47, emphasis added).

Before we discuss the specific deity of Masonry, we will first show that, despite its claim to accept and honor other religions, Masonry really teaches that all religions are worshiping the *same* God—rather than the God of any specific religion. That is, when the Muslim thinks he is worshiping Allah, he really isn't. When the Christian thinks he is worshiping the God of the Bible, he really isn't.

A Universal God

There can be no doubt that the Masonic rituals teach every Mason he is to serve and obey "God." In the lower degrees of the Blue Lodge, Masons of all particular religious persuasions must subscribe to a belief in God, who is vaguely described and named in such a way that members of almost any religion would be able to retain their own views of God by ascribing the names and descriptions to their own deity. For example, in the first degree he is called "the Almighty Father of the Universe." In the second degree he is, in addition, called "the Grand Geometrician of the Universe" (54:58) and "the Grand Artificer of the Universe" (54:82). In the third degree this deity is called "the Supreme Grand Architect of the Universe," "the Ideal Good and the Ideal Beauty," and "the Master Workman of the Universe" (57:106-108).

But it is also clear in these degrees that Masonry is referring to what it believes is the one true God. The opening prayer given in the Tennessee monitor reads, "Great Architect of the Universe, *in Thy name* we have assembled and *in Thy name* we desire to proceed in all our doings" (65:1, emphasis added). Masons of all religions—Buddhists, Hindus, Muslims, Jews, Christians, Mormons, Taoists, Shintoists, and so on, all are instructed to swear by and pray to this God.

As Alan Roberts, author of *The Craft and Its Symbols,* points out concerning "The Great Architect of the Universe,"

> This is the Freemasons' special name for God, because He is universal. He belongs to all men regardless of their religious persuasion. All wise men acknowledge His authority. In his private devotions a Mason will pray to Jehovah, Mohammed, Allah, Jesus, or the Deity of his choice. In a Masonic Lodge, however, the Mason will find the name of his Deity *within* the Great Architect of the Universe (as cited in 168:46, emphasis added).

Masonry teaches that if men call God by different names and define him differently, it is only because they don't know any better. They are doing this in ignorance because of the spiritual darkness in them. Masonry claims it can remove this darkness by revealing to them such truths as that all men actually worship the one true God. Thus, however highly developed and firmly held a religious belief the initiate brings to Masonry, he is nonetheless taught he is "in a state of darkness" and it is only through Masonry that he will be "brought to the light" (55:17). Masons are free to read their particular deities into the ritual, but that same ritual *excludes* those deities as being the one true God.

If Masons call God by many different names, and yet according to the first degree (65:13-14) are erecting a temple for the one "true" God to dwell within them, then Masonry must logically believe that all Masons are worshiping the same God. In the second degree of Masonry, all Masons, whatever their individual religious belief, are further informed they are "under obligation to pay that rational homage to the Deity which at once constitutes our duty and our happiness" (65:44). If all Masons are under spiritual duty to pay homage to this deity, then again, Masonry must expect all of its members to be worshiping the same God.

Finally, the Masonic doctrines of the universal fatherhood of God and brotherhood of man by definition must emphasize that all Masons really worship the same deity, whoever He is. Masons are told that all men are Sons of the One Father in Heaven—the Great Architect or Geometer of the Universe—and therefore all men are really spiritual brothers. Because it is claimed that all men are worshiping the one true God, Masonry concludes that men of all religious faiths should eventually come to associate the God of their particular religion with the God of Masonry.

24

Do Masons Teach that the One True God Is the God of Masonry?

Masonic rituals and authorities teach that there is a supreme God beyond standard religious concepts (172:198-201; 174:40-45). This deity that all men worship in ignorance is the God of Masonry. The Masonic allegiance to the Great Architect of the Universe is made evident by Martin Wagner, an early authority on Masonry:

> It is faith in this deity that, as a prerequisite for membership, is demanded at the door of the lodge of every candidate for Masonic honors. It is this deity in whose name the covenant is made, and who is invoked for help to keep it inviolate. It is to him that the prayers in the lodge are addressed,...whose praises are sung in Masonic odes and whose divinity is extolled. It is to him that Masonic altars are built, priests consecrated, sacrifices made, temples erected and solemnly dedicated. This Great Architect of

the Universe is the "one God" in Freemasonry and besides
him there is no other in that institution. Freemasonry as
such knows no deity save the Great Architect of the Universe (16:292-293).

As Pike's *Liturgy of the Scottish Rite* declares,

> The Supreme, Self-existent, Eternal, All-wise, All-powerful,
> infinitely Good, Pitying, Beneficent, and Merciful Creator
> and Preserver of the Universe *was the same, by whatever
> name he was called,* to the intellectual and enlightened men
> of all nations (93:162, as cited in 168:143, emphasis added).

Progression in Knowledge

As we noted earlier, initiates are promised they will learn who
God is. In the thirteenth degree of the Scottish Rite (Royal Arch of
Solomon), initiates are promised that they will be "learning the
true nature and attributes of the Deity" (197:157). After different
names of the deity are cited, the candidate is told that these are the
different names of "the one true God" (196).

In the Scottish Rite, degrees 19 through 30 are termed "The
Council of Kadosh." This council seeks "to explain as clearly and
as accurately as possible the nature of Deity and the relationship
between Him and mankind" (177:157-58).

In the twentieth degree of the Scottish Rite (Master of the
Symbolic Lodge), we are told concerning "Yah-balin," the second
password of the degree,

> If correctly written, it is a compound of...Yu or Yah-u...
> Baal or Bal or Bel, and Om, thus combining the names of
> the Hebrew, Phoenician and Hindu deities, to indicate that
> *they are in reality the same* (198:151, emphasis added).

In the fourteenth degree of the Scottish Rite (Perfect Elu),
Albert Pike stated the following:

> Masonry, around whose altars the Christian, the Hebrew,
> the Moslem, the Brahman, the followers of Confucius and

Zoroaster, can assemble as brethren and unite in prayer to the one God who is above all the Baalim, must needs leave it to each of its Initiates to look for the foundation of his faith and hope to the written scriptures of his own religion (26:226).

In illustration of this progression in knowledge, consider the meaning of the term *Baalim*. Who are the Baalim? Pike defines the term as the nations' varying concepts of God—idols and false gods that are found in religions outside of Masonry. These false gods are considered dim reflections of the one true Masonic God, the Supreme Architect, that Masonry reveals (51,V:51-52). Pike taught that Masonry believed "there is but one true religion, one dogma, *one legitimate belief*" (16:285, emphasis added).

In essence, in an evolving process through its degrees, Masonry exchanges a candidate's incomplete God for Masonry's true God. The individual Mason may think he is worshiping his particular God in Masonry—for example, the Christian may think he is worshiping the God of the Bible—but that is a serious miscalculation. Masonry considers Christians to be on the right track in worshiping a deity, but they are clearly wrong by specifically identifying the biblical Jehovah as the ultimate God. In fact, Masonry uses the Christian's belief in God to hoodwink him into worshiping a different God altogether:

> While it tacitly admits the existence of other gods in allowing its disciples to hold their private views, it does so on the theory that these god-ideas are perversions and corruptions of its own theistic conceptions and which it aims to correct....It reduces all monotheistic deities to one and the same thing as its Great Architect, and all the great religions as identical with itself (16:289,336, see 16:30).*

---

* In fact, Masonry's syncretism has eclectic elements. Thus, some Masons' description of God as Creator, Preserver, and Destroyer (83:77) is similar to Hindu conceptions; Masonry's stress on God's absolute unity and His transcendence over against His immanence is similar to the Muslim concept of God; Masonry's deism and pantheism are common to other religions; and so on.

Reeducation About the One True God

From the foregoing, we might expect Masonry, at least in the higher degrees, to actually oppose other concepts of God that conflict with its own. In fact, Masonry believes it alone possesses the truth about God and that every other concept of God is false. As a result, Masonry stresses the importance of education—"the capability of man to reach a higher level of perfection through education and training," in the words of the Pennsylvania Grand Chaplain (120:7). Masonry is fundamentally a religious training and reeducation—specifically, indoctrination into the unique theology of Masonry, including its own specific deity. This can be seen in the following two points.

First, despite its alleged concern for an individual's religion, *Masonry does not care by what name the candidates refer to God.* At the level of initiation, all that matters is that they believe in some god. Masonic authority Carl Claudy emphasizes that the Mason

> must declare his faith in a Supreme Being before he may be initiated. But note that he is not required to say, then or ever, what God. He may name him as he will, think of him as he pleases; make him impersonal law or personal and anthropomorphic; Freemasonry cares not....God, Great Architect of the Universe, Grand Artificer, Grand Master of the Grand Lodge Above, Jehovah, Allah, Buddha, Vishnu, Shiva, or Great Geometer (60,II:110).

Elsewhere, another authority teaches, "A belief in God is essential to a Mason, but...any god will do, so [long as] He is your God" (51,IV:32). Consider also words of "Freemasonry...asks no questions as to what God, nor even what kind of a god. Freemasonry cares not" (55:8-9).

Second, *what specific deity do Masons worship?* Masonic ritual and authorities provide some information allowing one to construct certain basics about the Masonic deity.

- *He is ultimately unknowable and unapproachable*—a veiled deity who hides himself within all religions where he is but dimly revealed. He reveals himself most specifically (though not completely) in Masonry. And even in Masonry, not so much in the lower degrees and to every Mason, as in the higher degrees and to those who become enlightened spiritually through serious Masonic study. The truly enlightened Mason "knows" God more than anyone else on earth, insofar as that is possible.

- *He is universal* and not restricted to the specific theology of any religion, except that of Masonry.

- *He has certain attributes or characteristics common to the deity*—infinity, eternality, omnipotence, and so on. He is transcendent and unitarian (as in Islam), not trinitarian (as in Christianity)—though Pike did use a triad to describe him. He is not impersonal or monistic (as in Hinduism), but he may contain within himself pantheistic or polytheistic tendencies or elements. Because of his strong association with kabbalism, gnosticism, and the ancient mystery religions, he is also clearly a pagan and pre-Christian deity (172:215-322).*

This is hardly the God of Christian faith. Just as Masonry has claimed it does not teach a system of salvation, but does; just as it claims it is not a religion, but is; just as it claims it reverences the

---

* In regard to this point, our book *The Secret Teachings of the Masonic Lodge* documents a connection between the Masonic Lodge, kabbalism, and other forms of occultism and spiritism, such as Rosicrucianism and hermetic philosophy. For instance, Mackey is only one Masonic authority who concludes that kabbalism is "intimately connected with the symbolic science of Freemasonry" (90:325). The twenty-fourth degree of the Scottish Rite (Prince of the Tabernacle) frankly declares, "Masonry is the Gnosis" (168:184, citing Pike's *Liturgy of the Scottish Rite*, part 4). We also concluded, "Masonry remains the daughter of the [ancient] mystery religions, even in ways that most Masons do not suspect" (172:253). Tsoukalas concurs (168:90), and Wagner's scholarly tome, *Freemasonry: An Interpretation*, reveals that Freemasonry is actually a thoroughgoing restoration of the pagan mysteries of ancient fertility and sun-worship cults. He concludes, perhaps not surprisingly, that the "Great Architect of the Universe" is simply a personification of the "generative principle" in nature, and even that many symbols of the Lodge are phallic in nature.

Bible, but doesn't; Masonry also claims that the God of Masonry and the God of Christianity are the same God—which it knows is a false claim, otherwise it would not oppose specific Christian beliefs. But supposedly, once we dismiss the errors of Christian theology and understand God as he truly is according to Masonic belief, then we can understand the truth. Christians who hold to specific theological or biblical views of God do so in ignorance, but Masonry will enlighten them.

25

DOES MASONRY SPECIFICALLY REJECT THE CHRISTIAN GOD? (204)

The Masonic Great Architect of the Universe appears more like the Aristotelian "First Cause" than the personal God who has revealed Himself in the Bible (199:43).

—*A STUDY OF FREEMASONRY,* HOME MISSION BOARD, SOUTHERN BAPTIST CONVENTION

Many declarations rejecting the Christian God can be found in authoritative Masonic writings and ritual. Coil, for example, argues that "monotheism...violates Masonic principles, for it requires belief in a specific kind of Supreme Deity" (95:517). Of course, at this point he has just excluded the God of the Bible. Albert Pike warns, "If our conceptions of God are those of the ignorant, narrow-minded, and vindictive Israelite...we feel that it is an affront and an indignity to Him" (174:46-56).

What Pike and other leading Masons have taught about God in the higher degrees of Masonry has little to do with the God of the Bible (172:108-26). For example, Pike categorized the God of Scripture as a false god and an idol when he wrote, "Every religion and every conception of God is idolatrous, insofar as it is imperfect, and as it substitutes a feeble and temporary idea in the shrine of that Undiscoverable Being" (26:516; see 26:226,295-296). In *Coil's Masonic Encyclopedia,* all men in the Lodge are told they must decide between the inferior Christian God or the one true God of Masonry:

> Men have to decide whether they want a God like the ancient Hebrew Jahweh, a partisan, tribal God, with whom they can talk and argue and from whom they can hide if necessary, or a boundless, eternal, universal, undenominational, and international, Divine Spirit, so vastly removed from the speck called man, that He cannot be known, named, or approached. So soon as man begins to laud his God and endow him with the most perfect human attributes such as justice, mercy, beneficence, etc., the Divine essence is depreciated and despoiled....The Masonic test [for admission] is a Supreme Being, and any qualification added is an innovation and distortion (95:516-517).

If Masonry specifically rejects the God of Christianity, though, how can it claim to be the tried and tested friend of Christian faith? Further, if it offers an unknowable, unapproachable, and undiscoverable God *beyond* the different concepts of God found in other religions, how can it logically ask the men of *any* religion to join its lodges?

Masonry does this because it seeks to develop a worldwide religious brotherhood beyond the sectarian religious beliefs of mankind. To further this goal it must at one level accept all religions while simultaneously pointing and leading to a "higher" truth beyond separatist religion—a truth Masons believe is capable of uniting all men in a common universal brotherhood. Thus, at one level, Masonry must encourage members of all different religions to pray to and worship their own respective gods—Brahma, Krishna, Allah, Brahman, Buddha, Jehovah, Vishnu, Jesus, and so on. This is the means by which Masonry can appeal to the members of all the different religions in the world.

But in their own beliefs, Masons cannot all be praying to the same God because all these gods are different in nature and in what they expect of men. The Masonic doctrine of the spiritual fatherhood of God and brotherhood of man is only valid if there really is some larger God beyond the contradictory lesser gods that men worship. So on the one hand Masonry claims it is an organization of tolerance that accepts the different religions of men; on the other hand, it offers a supreme God—supposedly the one true God that all men are really praying to—who is beyond the inferior, primitive concepts of individual religion, whether Christian, Hindu, Islamic, or Buddhist, or what have you (164:18). Masonry gives religion at one level but takes it away at another. At the lower level it is idolatrous, at the higher levels syncretistic.

26

IS THE GOD OF MASONRY UNAPPROACHABLE AND UNKNOWABLE?

Masonry says to its Initiates this: "God is One;
Unapproachable, Single, Eternal and Unchanging....
There is but one God, infinite and incomprehensible,
to whom no human attribute can be properly assigned,
even when imagined to be infinite" (51,V:51).

This authority's teaching is a further illustration that the God of the Bible is rejected in the Lodge. Masonry claims God is "unapproachable." To the contrary, the Bible teaches that God can be approached by men (through Christ) and that it is God's will that men do so. In Masonry, men are told that God is "single." But the Bible teaches that God is a trinitarian being. Finally, Masonry says that God does not have personal emotions. He "is incapable of anger" (26:718).

In certain ways, Masonic belief is similar to what is known as *deism*, which involves accepting a belief in God apart from revelation. (Some Masons are deists, others are not.) In Masonry, nature is the primary revealer of God, and this suggests why the scriptures of all faiths are held to be merely symbolic. Usually there is a secondary idea behind deism: that although God is the Creator of the world, He pretty much leaves the world to itself:

> In its doctrine concerning the revelation of God, the institution is deistic. It denies that the deity has made any supernatural revelation of himself, or of his will to man. It rejects the Bible as supernatural revelation. It recognizes no revelation except that set forth in nature (16:284).

> Nature is the great Teacher of man; for it is the Revelation of God. It neither dogmatizes nor attempts to tyrannize by compelling to a particular creed or special interpretation (26:64).

Further, there are even *pantheistic* conceptions of the Masonic deity implied in the higher degrees. For example, Masonry accepts a particular form of *pantheism* (that all is God and God is all) called *panentheism* (that the universe is God's "body"):

> In its doctrines concerning the divine immanence Freemasonry is decidedly pantheistic, partaking of the various shades of that view of the divine. God (the Great Architect) is the great "soul" of the universe, and the universe is the garment in which he is clothed (16:286).

> The Masonic view of the revelation of God, in the lower degrees, is deistic, but in the higher degrees it becomes pantheistic. The writings of Garrison, Buck, Pike, and other eminent Masons show this unmistakably. It is this peculiar pantheistic conception of deity which has passed from India through the secret doctrines of the Kabbalah into modern speculative Freemasonry....In Masonry, a god distinct from the life of nature, has no existence (16:309-10).

Summing Up

Apart from personal revelation, little that is concrete can be said about God beyond the basic, universally accepted attributes of an infinite deity. It seems that the only two absolutely required characteristics for the Masonic deity are 1) absolute impassiveness—that is, complete insusceptibility to being affected by any outside agent—and (2) absolute unknowability. In contrast to the God of the Bible, the Masonic God cannot be offended by men, nor can he really ever be known by men.

To Masonry, the Christian belief is really an "inferior" view of God that Christians hold in their spiritual naiveté (16:289). Is it permissible for a Christian Mason to hold to a Christian view of God? Initially, yes. Is this the true God? Definitely not. As a Christian learns more and more of Masonic teachings, he is faced with a conflict between the so-called inferior view of God he was taught as a Christian and the superior, "more grand and sublime" Masonic conception of deity. The result? The Christian begins to think that the biblical God is an inferior representation of the One True God—which may impact every area of his spiritual life.

27

DOES MASONRY REJECT THE CHRISTIAN CONCEPT OF GOD'S TRIUNE NATURE?

The trinity of Deity belongs to no single religion (177:228).

—HUTCHENS, *A BRIDGE TO LIGHT*

Whenever Masonry describes God, it usually describes Him as "one," "single," or "unitarian." It must do so—otherwise, it will offend Masons who are not Christians (such as Jews and Muslims, who reject the Trinity). As the proceedings of the Grand Lodge of Texas admonish, "No phrase or terms should be used in a Masonic service that would arouse sectarian feelings or wound the religious sensibilities of any Freemason" (19:37). Newton refers to the "chief mission" of Masonry as "the preservation of belief in the unity of God" (77:164). As one author put it, "Masonry holds and teaches that with all and above all there is God, not essentially a Christian triune God"(19:37).

One source notes that Christian Masons are permitted to believe in "a symbolical triune essence" but only as a "subsidiary and secondary" belief after faith in the Masonic God (12:234). Interestingly, though, in the higher degrees there are expressions of belief in a triad, or "Masonic Trinity." Pike's *Liturgy of the Scottish Rite* refers to "the Masonic Trinity—Three Potencies of one Essence" (part 4, as cited in 168:190). His *Magnum Opus* declares, "Behold THE TRUE MASONIC TRINITY: the UNIVERSAL SOUL; the THOUGHT in the Soul; the WORD, or the Thought expressed: the THREE IN ONE, of a Trinitarian Ecossias[sic]" (XXVI,36, as cited in 168:190; see 26:575). Clearly, however, this belief is opposed to the Christian concept of God's triune nature.

28

Do Masons Refer to Their God Using Names of Heathen Gods That Are Condemned in the Bible?

As noted earlier, Masonry comprises a modern revival of ancient pagan mystery religion. The Texas monitor, for instance, acknowledges that "the most learned among Masonic scholars conclude that Masonry is of very ancient origin, and is in some aspects, the modern successor of, and heir to...the Temples of India, Chaldea, Greece and Rome, as well as the basic doctrines of the Essenes, Gnostics and other mystic Orders" (69:xiv). Therefore,

> every candidate for the Mysteries of Masonry, at the proper time and in an appropriate manner, should be taught the truth that the rite of Initiation means much more than a formal ceremonial progress through the Degrees....Initiation is to be attained only after real labor, deep study, profound meditation, extensive research and a constant practice of those virtues which will open a true path to moral, intellectual, and spiritual illumination" (69:xv-xvi).

In other words, the initiate is to be informed as to the deeper pagan meanings of Masonic ritual.

One of the most astounding aspects of the deeper parts of the ritual is the subject of this chapter. It is not until the Royal Arch Degree of the York Rite that the Mason is finally told the true name of God. Before this, the Mason is told that the real name of God has been lost. The Royal Arch Mason, however, is told that the secret name of the Masonic deity is *Jabulon*. Masons who have taken only the first three degrees of the Blue Lodge are not aware that the Great Architect of the Universe is also Jabulon (12:243; 19:32; 4:10). In *The Brotherhood*, an exposé of Masonry, Stephen Knight reported, "I have spoken to no less than 57 long-standing Royal Arch Freemasons" who, he says, were happy to discuss all aspects of Masonry with him. "However, all but four lost their self-assurance and composure when I said, 'What about Jah-bul-on?'" All of the Masons attempted to move the conversation to another topic. "If I insisted on returning to Jah-bul-on, almost invariably the interview would be unceremoniously terminated"(12:237).

According to Knight, even Albert Pike had a problem with the word:

> No man or body of men can make me accept as a sacred word, as a symbol of the infinite and eternal Godhead, a mongrel word, in part composed of the name of an accursed and beastly heathen god, whose name has been for more than 2,000 years an appellation of the devil (12:236-237).

Here we agree with Pike, and one thing is certain: In the ritual of the Royal Arch degree, Masonry connects the one true and righteous God of the Bible with the evil and pagan deities of the ancients. Every Royal Arch Mason is told that the true name for the God he has been praying to throughout the different degrees of Masonry is *Jehovah* joined with *Baal* (the ancient Canaanite god) and apparently *Osiris* (an Egyptian mystery god). Wagner observed,

> In this compound name an attempt is made to show by a coordination of divine names...the unity, identity and harmony of the Hebrew, Assyrian and Egyptian god-ideas, and the harmony of the Royal Arch religion with these ancient religions. This Masonic "unity of God" is peculiar. It is the doctrine that the different names of gods, Brahma, Jehovah, Baal, Bel, Om, On, etc., all denote the generative principle, in that all religions are essentially the same in their ideas of the divine (16:338-339).

Coil's Masonic Encyclopedia agrees: "Jah, Bel, and On appear in the American ritual of the Royal Arch degree on the supposition that Jah was the Syriac name of god, Bel (Baal), the Chaldean, and On, the Egyptian" (95:516).

What Is the Concern with the Name *Jabulon?*

The second god mentioned in the composite name Ja-bul-on—"Baal,"—is the wicked and vile Canaanite nature deity (see 111; 112; 113; 114; 115). We have selected this deity for mention because it is the god whose name appears on the Masonic altar.

> There is no dispute between Freemasons and their fiercest critics that both the word Jehovah and the composite word, Jahbulon, appear on the altar, on top of which is inscribed a circle, containing a triangle. Around the circle is inscribed the name JEHOVAH and on the three sides of the triangle the letters JAH BUL ON....To all of this must be added the third and final feature of the top of the pedestal: the Hebrew characters set at the angles of the triangle: Alif, Beth, and Lamed, each of which is said to have reference to the deity or to some divine attribute. [Here the writer quotes a Masonic source.] "Take each combination [of the letters] with the whole, and it will read this: Ab Bal, [meaning] Father, Lord: Al Bal, Word, Lord; Lab Bal, Spirit, Lord." The obvious result of such juggling of the

Hebrew characters is to emphasize the formation of Bal, the name of a Semitic deity bitterly opposed by Elijah and the later Hebrew prophets; to associate this name in any way with that of Jehovah would have deeply shocked them (102:27,29).

Why would associating Baal's name with Jehovah have shocked the prophets? Because Baal was condemned by God as a false idol, in whose name incredible evil was done. It would have shocked the prophets in the same way it shocks us when we read of certain modern cults teaching that Satan is God.

In fact, as Pike noted, historically Baal has been another name for the devil. The god Baal was sufficiently satanic that Jesus used the name of Baal in an extended manner for Satan himself, as did all the Jews of His time. *Beelzeboul* is the New Testament name for Satan based on the Old Testament *Baalzebub* (115:298; see Luke 11:15-19; Matthew 10:25-27).

Not surprisingly, history records that Baal worship was one of the most evil systems of idolatry to be found in the ancient world. It repeatedly led God's people astray into the worst kinds of sin and vice, including the practice of self-mutilation (1 Kings 18:28), ritual prostitution (Judges 2:17; Jeremiah 7:9; Amos 2:7), and even the sacrificing (ritual murder) of children (Jeremiah 19:4-5,15). Just to illustrate, consider a Scripture passage (one of more than 50 in the Old Testament) that indicates how evil Baal worship was, how destructive its influence on the people of God was, and how much God abhorred this false deity:

> Because they have forsaken Me and have made this an alien place and have burned sacrifices in it to other gods...and because they have filled this place with the blood of the innocent and have built the high places of Baal to burn their sons in the fire as burnt offerings to Baal, a thing which I never commanded or spoke of, nor did it ever enter my mind; therefore,...behold, I am about to bring on this city and all its towns the entire calamity that I have

declared against it; because they have stiffened their necks so as to not heed My words (Jeremiah 19:4,5,15).

God condemned Israel's evil in choosing Baal, calling this practice idolatry. The first commandment reads, "You shall have no other gods before me." The biblical God will have no other gods before Him because such gods do not exist—only devils who lead people into idolatry and sin. Lifting up one such as Baal to be equal to God becomes perhaps the most hideous form of idolatry. As a Committee of the General Synod of the Church of England concluded,

> JAHBULON (whether it is a name or description), which appears in all the rituals, must be considered blasphemous: in Christian theology the name of God (Yahweh/Jehovah) must not be taken in vain, nor can it be replaced by an amalgam of the names of pagan deities (102:30).

29

Can Christian Masons Follow the Biblical God and Also Believe Masonic Teachings About Deity?

The entire thrust of both the Old and New Testament revelation is to warn men against the consequences of worshiping false gods. Idolatry sends men to hell. Jesus declared, "It is written, 'You shall worship the Lord your God and serve Him only'" (Luke 4:8). God warned,

> You shall fear only the LORD your God; and you shall worship Him....You shall not follow other gods, any of the gods of the peoples who surround you, for the LORD your God in the midst of you is a jealous God; otherwise the anger of the LORD your God will be kindled against you, and He will wipe you off the face of the earth (Deuteronomy 6:13-15).

No other God is like the true God. "Who is like You among the gods, O LORD? Who is like You, majestic in holiness, awesome in praises, working wonders?" (Exodus 15:11). "Great is the LORD, and greatly to be praised; He also is to be feared above all the gods. For all the gods of the peoples are idols, but the LORD made the heavens....Tremble before Him, all the earth;...for He is coming to judge the earth" (1 Chronicles 16:25-26,30,33).

Jesus declared, "This is eternal life, that they may *know* You, the *only* true God, and Jesus Christ whom You have sent" (John 17:3). We can know that the God of the Bible is the only true God because only He has revealed Himself in history through powerful and persuasive evidence. This evidence includes predicting the future many times over in His revelation, the Bible; incarnating Himself and performing unparalleled miracles in the person of Christ; and, thus incarnate, dying on a cross but rising from the dead. What other God ever did things like this in real history? There is none because other gods are only concepts, not truly existent entities. God Himself declares, "I, even I, am the LORD; and there is no savior besides Me....I am the LORD, and there is no other; besides Me there is no God" (Isaiah 43:11; 45:5).

If there is only one true God—the God of the Bible—Masonry is encouraging people to engage in idolatry and is promoting belief in a multitude of false gods. "God is a spirit; and those who worship Him must worship in spirit and *truth*" (John 4:24).

In sum, Masonry 1) rejects the true God; 2) permits, at one level, a variety of gods of different faiths to occupy its altar according to individual Masonic belief; 3) at a higher level in the Scottish Rite, officially defines God as the Masonic deity, whom it encourages all men to worship and who is itself a false god; and 4) in the York Rite associates this God with the secret name *Jabulon*—a joining together of the biblical God and evil, heathen deities.

In conclusion, Christian Masons have to wrestle with what the Bible teaches about God, what Masonry teaches about God, the difference between the two—and the difference it makes. In the words of Jesus, "No one can serve two masters; for either he will hate the one and love the other, or he will be devoted to one and despise the other" (Matthew 6:24).

Masonry and Jesus Christ

30

Does Masonry Delete the Name of Christ from Its Prayers and Scripture Quotations?

In general, Masonry believes that Christ was an enlightened man, although not unique deity as the Bible teaches. For example, for many Masons, Jesus is referred to as "the greatest of all Spiritual Masons" (202). Some Masons have also expressed the opinion that the biblical story of Christ constitutes a corrupted version of ancient pagan legends. Mason's unwillingness to "offend" non-Christians and their unbiblical views of Christ help explain their approach to Jesus in the rituals.

Thus, Masonry deletes the name of Jesus Christ when the ritual cites biblical passages so as to not offend non-Christian Masons. For example:

Reference	Masonry	The Bible
1 Peter 2:5	"…to offer up spiritual sacrifices acceptable to God" (31:181,184).	"…to offer up spiritual sacrifices acceptable to God *through Jesus Christ.*"

2 Thessalonians 3:6	"Now we command you, brethren, that ye withdraw yourselves from every brother that walketh disorderly, and not after the tradition which he received of us" (68:206; see 31:181).	"Now we command you, brethren, *in the name of our Lord Jesus Christ,* that you keep away from every brother who leads an unruly life and not according to the tradition which you received from us."
2 Thessalonians 3:12	"Now them that are such, we command and exhort, that with quietness they work, and eat their own bread" (68:206).	"Now such persons we command and exhort *in the Lord Jesus Christ* to work in quiet fashion and eat their own bread."

Steven Tsoukalas points out that "assorted Masonic services clearly evidence the expunging of Christ from the biblical text and the wrenching of biblical texts from their proper contexts" (168: 119,121,173). Among other problems, "Through selective, inaccurate, and out-of-context citing of the Scriptures, the Scottish Rite ritual takes passages that are intended to exalt and refer to Jesus Christ and makes them refer to the 'common Father of all mankind'" (168:181).

While Masonry is unwilling to offend non-Christians, it does seem willing to offend Christians by deleting the name of Christ when the ritual cites a scripture in which Christ's name is mentioned.

31

ARE PRAYERS IN THE NAME OF CHRIST
FORBIDDEN IN THE LODGE?

Almost without exception, again in harmony with a policy of nonoffense, Masonry prohibits the giving of prayers in the name of Christ in the Lodge (178). For example, in Mackey's *Masonic Ritualist*, there are almost 30 sample prayers given for different Masonic occasions, and not one is offered in the name of Christ (153; see 10:68). However, the Christian is to pray to God the Father in the name of Christ, not as a formal procedure, but out of thanksgiving, recognizing all that Christ is. For Christ, he is to labor in fervent prayer, to continue in prayer, to strive in prayer, and so on (Colossians 3:17; John 14:13; 20:31; Ephesians 5:20; 6:18; Romans 12:12; 15:30; Philippians 4:6; Colossians 4:2,12; 1 Thessalonians 5:17).

The *Maryland Master Mason* magazine asserts the following as Masonic practice:

> All prayers in Mason lodges should be directed to the one deity to whom all Masons refer as the Grand Architect of the Universe....Prayers in the lodges should be closed with expressions such as "in the Most Holy and precious name we pray," using no additional words which would be in conflict with the religious beliefs of those present at meetings (March 1973 issue, as cited in 21:112).

Consider the following real-life example of what happens to the untested Christian Mason who attempts to offer a prayer in the name of Jesus Christ:

> The Commander of the Guard called me aside and rebuked me sharply. He said....I had ended the prayer "in Christ's holy name." For that, he said, I would be reported!....I was called in to see the Secretary of the Scottish Rite [who was a Christian Scientist] about my unsatisfactory performance.

He was nice about it, but told me that I was never to end a prayer "in Jesus' name" or "in Christ's name." He said, "Make your prayers universal" (20:72).

If Masons want to prohibit the use of the name of Christ so as to not offend anyone, that's their business. But then they should not promise Christians in the Masonic ritual itself that there is nothing in Masonry that will offend them or the duties they owe to their God.

<hr>

32

DOES MASONRY REQUIRE THAT CHRISTIANS DISOBEY JESUS CHRIST BY PROHIBITING ANY DISCUSSION OF HIM DURING LODGE ACTIVITY?

Masonry prohibits the Christian from talking about Christ in any fashion in the lodge. The Texas monitor, along with many others, stresses that Masonry is correct in "forbidding all sectarian discussion within its lodge rooms" (69:89).

The *charges* (regulations) of Freemasonry adopted in 1723 instructed the Christian Mason to keep his own personal religious opinions to himself:

> Though in ancient Times Masons were charged in every Country to be of the Religion of that Country or nation, whatever it was, yet 'tis now thought more expedient only to oblige them to that Religion in which all men agree [Masonry], leaving their particular Opinions to themselves (96,I:192).

> Albert Pike asserts in his discussion of the tenth degree of the Scottish Rite,

> No man truly obeys the Masonic law who merely tolerates those whose religious opinions are opposed to his own.... The Mason's creed goes further than that. No man, it holds, has any right in any way to interfere with the religious belief of another. It holds that each man is absolutely sovereign as to his own belief (26:167).

Notice, however, that Pike was not speaking merely of activity within the lodge, but of religious belief in general, anywhere. Previsioning modern political correctness, he argued that there is no right, period, to speak to others, anywhere, about Christ because this is to "interfere" with their personal sovereign religious beliefs. Further, if one truly understands the nature of the God of Masonry, there is simply no need to speak about Jesus, who is nothing special to begin with—though of course it is permitted to speak and teach other Masons about the Grand Architect of the Universe and His interests.

The Christian, however, is commanded by Jesus Christ Himself to be a witness of His love to all men, wherever they are. Jesus commanded His disciples, "Go therefore and make disciples of all the nations, baptizing them in the name of the Father and the Son and the Holy Spirit, teaching them to observe all that I commanded you; and lo, I am with you always, even to the end of the age" (Matthew 28:19-20).

All people, including Masons, are in need of the good news. The apostle Paul taught, "I am under compulsion; for woe is me if I do not preach the gospel....For though I am free from all men, I have made myself a slave to all, so that I might win more" (1 Corinthians 9:16,19). Paul further writes,

> I solemnly charge you in the presence of God and of Christ Jesus, who is to judge the living and the dead, and by His appearing and His kingdom: preach the word; be ready in season and out of season; reprove, rebuke, exhort, with great patience and instruction (2 Timothy 4:1-4).

33

DOES MASONRY BESTOW CHRIST'S DIVINE TITLES AND OFFICES UPON UNSAVED MEN IN THE LODGE?

Despite the exclusion of Christ from Lodge ritual and discussion, somewhat paradoxically, the divine offices and titles of

Christ *are* given to Masons or used by them as Masonic pass-words. Among these are "My beloved Son," "I AM THAT I AM," "Melchizedek," "Immanuel," "Jehovah," "Adonai," and others.

The Divine Name, "I AM"

In Exodus 3:14, God called Himself by the special name "I Am." "This is my name forever, and this is my memorial-name to all generations" (Exodus 3:15). God also warned, "You shall not misuse the name of the LORD your God, for the LORD will not hold anyone guiltless who misuses his name" (20:7 NIV).

Jesus also repeatedly referred to Himself as the "I Am"— thereby appropriating to Himself the very name of God, indicating His unique deity. For example, He warned that others would come and claim to be the "I Am" and would deceive many: "See to it that no one misleads you. Many will come in My name, saying, 'I Am He!' and will mislead many" (Mark 13:5-6).

The Masonic Lodge, though, has reduced God's name to a password. Masons also apply the "I Am" title of God and Christ to themselves in their response during the ritual of the Royal Arch (seventh) degree of the York Rite:

> Principal Sojourner—We will go up. Companions, you will follow me; our password is, "I AM THAT I AM" (58:234).
>
> Master of First Veil—How do you expect to enter here?
>
> Principal Sojourner—By a password that we received in Babylon.
>
> Master of First Veil—Give it to me.
>
> Principal Sojourner—I AM THAT I AM" (58:235).
>
> High Priest (to Captain of the Host)—Are you a Royal Arch Mason?
>
> Captain—"I am that I am" (58:252).

Because Jesus was God, it was right and proper for Him to refer to Himself using God's holy name. But for any man to apply God's name to himself is blasphemy.

Jehovah

The Scottish Rite uses the name "Jehovah" as a sacred word or password in the fifth, eighth, and twenty-third degrees. In addition, the word "Adonai" (Lord) is used in the fourth degree, and "Immanuel" is used in the nineteenth degree. Masons even have the name "Jaweh" on the Masonic jewel in the twenty-seventh degree (59,II:184).

The ancient Jews would not even speak the name of God aloud, and they would have looked with horror upon anyone who took God's name for himself or disgraced it as a password in a ritual.

The Title "The Son of God"

Manly Hall, a thirty-third-degree Mason, indirectly applies the title "Son of God" to all Master Masons in this instruction:

> For him [the Master Mason] the Heavens have opened and the Great Light has bathed him in its radiance....The voice [of God] speaks from the Heavens, its power thrilling the Master [Mason] until his own being seems filled with its divinity, saying, "This is my beloved Son, in whom I am well pleased" (35:55).

The Priest–King After the Order of Melchizedek

Manly Hall also teaches that the priestly office of Jesus is given to the Master Mason, who "is a Priest-King after the Order of Melchizedek, who is above the law....He wears the triple crown of the ancient magus [occult magician] for he is in truth the King of heaven, earth, and hell" (35:59).

The basis for this is found in Masonic ritual. During the initiation ceremony of the nineteenth (Grand Pontiff) degree of the Scottish Rite, the Thrice Puissant anoints the candidate with oil on the crown of his head and says: "Be thou a Priest forever, after the order of Melchizedek"....After receiving the password (Emmanuel) and the sacred word (Hallelujah), he is dressed in a robe of white linen and given a cordon (a ribbon or sash of honor worn across the breast) of crimson color (59,II:26-27).

All Christians who take this degree should realize that in accepting the office of "a Priest forever, after the order of Melchizedek," they have appropriated to themselves that which Jesus Christ alone possesses eternally: "It is declared: 'You are a priest forever, in the order of Melchizedek'" (Hebrews 7:17).

The One Worthy to Open the Seals

In the seventeenth degree of the Scottish Rite (the Knight of the East and West), in which the candidate symbolically becomes an Essene, he learns that he "becomes God's soldier to war against Fanaticism, Intolerance, Bigotry, Falsehood, [and so on]." At one point, using a reference to the book of Revelation where only Jesus is found worthy to open the book with the seven seals, "The Master [of the lodge] anoints him [the candidate] with oil and says, 'You are worthy to open the book with seven seals'" (Pike's *Liturgy of the Scottish Rite* and *The Magnum Opus*, XVII, 9, as cited in 168:164).*

Communion

A final example: In Christian belief, communion is a sacred commemoration of Christ's death on the cross for our sin. However in the thirtieth degree of the Scottish Rite, we discover a

---

* In addition, in the nineteenth degree of the Scottish Rite, the "Thrice Puissant" is portrayed as a kind of rival to Christ Himself. The parallels between the "Thrice Puissant" and Christ in the Masonic ritual are described by John Blanchard, former president of Wheaton College: "The Lodge Master is 'Thrice Puissant': personating Christ, who has 'all power.' The Master is 'seated on a throne and holds a Sceptre,' with the blue canopy of the heavens over him. This is Christ's rival....The degree itself, says Mackey,...'is founded on the mysteries of the Apocalypse,' which is 'the revelation of Jesus Christ' (Revelation 1:1). And his lodge members are 'clothed in white linen robes,' like attending Angels (Revelation 15:6); and on the jewel is engraved 'Alpha and Omega,' which is the title of Christ" (59,II:35).

different type of communion service. The Mason is present before an altar with a human skull and is solemnly warned of his obligations to Masonry. The Thrice Puissant Grand Master places the "candidate's hand on the skull" and then "they all drink from the same cup....They all break together the bread" (59,II:285).

34
———————

Does Masonry Deny the Deity of Jesus Christ?

So as not to offend others, Masonry teaches that Jesus Christ was a man only. Former Masonic leader Jim Shaw—a thirty-third-degree Mason, a Past Worshipful Master of the Blue Lodge, Past Master of all Scottish Rite bodies, and a Knight Commander of the Court of Honor—says that official Masonic doctrine teaches that "Jesus was just a man. He was one of the 'exemplars,' one of the great men of the past, but not divine and certainly not the only means of redemption of lost mankind" (20:126-127).

The Maundy Thursday ritual of the chapter of Rose Croix shows that Masonry is unwilling to accept the deity of Jesus Christ: "We meet this day to commemorate the death [of Jesus], not as inspired or divine, for this is not for us to decide" (20:127; see 91:75-77).

In essence, Masonry remolds Jesus into its own image "as an example of a great reformer laying down his life to free the oppressed from the tyranny of societal and spiritual ignorance" (168:167). Consider the teachings of *A Bridge to Light* by Rex R. Hutchens.* In the words of a Southern Baptist report,

> According to *A Bridge to Light*, Jesus of Nazareth was not
> unique. The book teaches that Jesus was just one messiah

———————

* This official publication was unanimously approved by the Scottish Rite Committee on Rituals and Ceremonial Forms. It is intended by its author to be a bridge between Albert Pike's commentaries on the Scottish Rite in *Morals and Dogma* and the actual ceremonies of the degrees, and its purpose is to help enlighten Masons about Pike's teachings. (While before all Scottish Rite candidates were once given the difficult-to-read *Morals and Dogma*, they are today offered *A Bridge to Light*.)

among the many messiahs found in the world's religions. Jesus is placed on the same level as the pagan deities Dionysus, Sosiosch, Krishna, and Osiris. "We see references to Dionysius [sic] of the Greeks, Sosiosch of the Persians, Krishna of the Hindus, Osiris of the Egyptians, Jesus of the Christians. The purpose of these varying cultures' messiahs was to find in human form a source of intercession with Deity; in particular one who, as a human, had been tempted and suffered the daily pangs of life and so could be expected to possess a particular sympathy and understanding; in a word, the messiah's expressed hope" (176).

The following Masonic writers favor the idea that God inwardly dwells within all humanity, making all men divine, regardless of belief. In his *Symbolism, or Mystic Masonry,* J.D. Buck wrote, "[Christian] theologians first made a fetish of the Impersonal Omnipresent Divinity; and then tore the Christos [latent divinity] from the hearts of all humanity in order to deify Jesus, that they might have a god-man peculiarly their own" (21:102). In a similar fashion, R. Swineburne Clymer, a high Mason, teaches in *The Mysticism of Masonry,*

> In deifying Jesus, the whole humanity is bereft of Christos as an eternal potency within every human soul, a latent (embryonic) Christ in every man. In thus deifying one man [Jesus], they have orphaned the whole of humanity [of its divinity] (21:102).

According to Masonry, an individual Christian Mason may choose to believe that Jesus was God and Savior of the world, but this is not Masonic truth. Indeed, those who consider themselves enlightened Masons hope that their unenlightened Christian brethren will some day realize that *all* their specific dogmas about Christ are in error. As we have previously quoted, Clausen emphasizes, "It is important to 'strip from all religions their orthodox tenets, legends, allegories and dogmas'" (94:157). In line with this,

Albert Pike asserted that Jesus was "a great teacher of morality"—but no more (26:525).

As we have seen, it is not true for Masons to say that Masonry does not offend anyone's religion. By teaching that Jesus was only a man, this is exactly what Masonry does to Christians. Because the unique nature and mission of Christ is denied by, for example, Hindus, Muslims, Buddhists, and Jews, in order to not offend these people, Masonry has little choice but to offend Christians.

35

DOES MASONRY DENY THE ROLE OF CHRIST AS SAVIOR AND TEACH THAT THE CHRISTIAN MESSAGE OF DIVINE REDEMPTION IS A CORRUPTION OF PAGAN STORIES?

In addition to denying Christ's deity, Masonry denies the biblical teaching that Jesus Christ is the world's only Redeemer and Savior from sin. Christianity is unique in critical ways, and one of these is that only Christianity proves—objectively, empirically, and in history—that God truly loves mankind:

> This is love, not that we loved God, but that He loved us and sent His Son to be the propitiation [atoning sacrifice] for our sins....We have seen and testify that the Father has sent the Son to be the Savior of the world (1 John 4:10,14).

> There is salvation in no one else; for there is no other name under heaven that has been given among men by which we must be saved (Acts 4:12).

Nowhere in Masonic literature will anyone find Jesus called God or see Him portrayed as the world's Savior who died for men's sin. To portray Him in such a light would "offend" some men—and again, Masonry hopes to offend none.

The necessity of Masonry's view of Christ springs from its fundamental doctrines, or "landmarks": the fatherhood of God, the brotherhood of man, and the immortality of the soul, all

Masonically interpreted. It follows from these doctrines that there is neither reason nor necessity that Jesus should be unique— either as to His Person (God) or His mission (Savior). Masonry teaches that man can expect a right standing with God by personal merit. All men can achieve eternal life regardless of their personal religious beliefs by being good men. As a result, there is no need for God to come in the flesh (Philippians 2:1-8) in order to die for the world's sin (John 3:16), because all men can be saved by their own efforts. As Tsoukalas observes,

> Throughout the rituals of the Scottish Rite there is no mention of *all* humanity's need for Christ's atonement. Nor does it correctly define the gospel….Jesus' laying down his life was an example of a great reformer sacrificing himself for oppressed humanity, for the cause of the Fatherhood of God and the Brotherhood of Man (168:168).

This is why Masonry excludes all particular biblical doctrines about Christ, such as His incarnation, unique teachings, redemptive mission, and physical resurrection. In fact, there is no important biblical truth about Jesus Christ that is affirmed by Masonry. Former Mason Edmond Ronayne concludes,

> Freemasonry "carefully excludes" the Lord Jesus Christ from the Lodge and chapter, repudiates his mediatorship, rejects his atonement, denies and disowns his gospel, frowns upon his religion and his church, ignores the Holy Spirit, and sets up for itself a spiritual empire, a religious theocracy, at the head of which it places the G.A.O.T.U.— the god of nature—and from which the one only living and true God is expelled by resolution (31:87).

Some Masons believe that the biblical teaching of Christ as God and Savior is merely a corruption of "similar," more "pure" stories in some of the earlier pagan religious traditions (20:127; 26:524; 21:102-103). These Masons believe that the New Testament is a corrupted version of such stories and that Christianity per se is false. In fact, they are offended that Christianity teaches that only Jesus is God because they prefer a more mystical Christ who teaches that all men are divine. For example, *Mystic Masonry and the Bible* (1975) offers an amalgamation of Christian mysticism, Theosophy, and occultism. The true "Christ" resides within all men as higher consciousness and is the means to encourage man toward occult development (28:19,33,47,90-91).

None of the above Masonic teachings about Christ agree with what Jesus taught about Himself and with what the Church has maintained for 2,000 years. Once again it must be asked, "If Masonry has such little regard for the teachings of Jesus, can it logically claim to be a 'tolerant' religion that is respectful of other beliefs?"

36

WHAT DOES THE BIBLE TEACH ABOUT JESUS CHRIST, AND WHAT DOES THIS MEAN FOR CHRISTIAN MASONS?

Masons who are Christians need to wrestle with what Jesus and the Bible teach and compare this with what Masonry teaches.

To begin, the Bible teaches that Jesus is the unique and only begotten Son of God—the only incarnation of God ever to appear (Philippians 2:1-9; John 1:1-14; 3:16,18). The Bible emphasizes that Jesus is not on the same level as merely human religious teachers. He is exalted far above every name and authority in all creation:

> God highly exalted Him, and bestowed on Him the name which is above every name, so that at the name of Jesus every knee will bow, of those who are in heaven and on earth and under the earth, and that every tongue will confess that Jesus Christ is Lord, to the glory of the Father (Philippians 2:9-11).

By Him all things were created, both in the heavens and on earth, visible and invisible, whether thrones or dominions or rulers or authorities—all things have been created by Him and for Him. He is before all things, and in Him all things hold together (Colossians 1:16-17).

Jesus Himself taught he was distinct from all others:

I am the Light of the world; he who follows me will not walk in darkness, but will have the light of life (John 8:12).

He who comes from above is above all (John 3:31).

If you continue in My word, then you are truly disciples of Mine; and you will know the truth, and the truth will make you free (John 8:31-32).

I am the way, and the truth, and the life; no one comes to the Father but through Me (John 14:6).

In addition, the Bible teaches that Jesus is deity. His teachings have infallible authority. Jesus is not merely an "exemplar" or one who had "good moral teachings"—He is God Himself:

In the beginning was the Word, and the Word was with God, and the Word was God....And the Word became flesh, and dwelt among us (John 1:1,14).

Jesus said to them, "Truly, truly, I say to you, before Abraham was born, I am" (John 8:58).

I and the Father are One (John 10:30).

He who has seen Me has seen the Father (John 14:9).

In Him all the fullness of Deity dwells in bodily form (Colossians 2:9).

Because Jesus Christ is God, He will one day judge all people from throughout history:

Not even the Father judges anyone, but He has given all judgment to the Son, so that all will honor the Son even as they honor the Father. He who does not honor the Son does not honor the Father who sent Him (John 5:22-23).

When the Son of Man comes in His glory, and all the angels with Him, then He will sit on His glorious throne. All the nations will be gathered before Him; and He will separate them from one another, as the shepherd separates the sheep from the goats....Then the King will say to those on His right, "Come, you who are blessed of My Father, inherit the kingdom prepared for you from the foundation of the world."...Then He will also say to those on His left, "Depart from Me, accursed ones, into the eternal fire which has been prepared for the devil and his angels."... These will go away into eternal punishment, but the righteous into eternal life (Matthew 25:31-34,41,46).

Both Jesus and the New Testament writers emphasize that He alone is the Savior of the world, whose death on the cross paid the penalty for human sin:

The Son of Man did not come to be served, but to serve, and to give His life a ransom for many (Matthew 20:28).

God so loved the world, that He gave His only begotten Son, that whoever believes in Him shall not perish, but have eternal life. For God did not send the Son into the world to judge the world, but that the world might be saved through Him. He who believes in Him is not judged; he who does not believe has been judged already, because he has not believed in the name of the only begotten Son of God (John 3:16-18).

Truly, truly, I say to you, he who hears My word, and believes Him who sent Me, has eternal life, and does not come into judgment, but has passed out of death into life (John 5:24).

Jesus answered and said to them, "This is the work of God, that you believe in Him whom He has sent" (John 6:29).

There is one God, and one mediator also between God and men, the man Christ Jesus, who gave Himself as a ransom for all, the testimony given at the proper time (1 Timothy 2:5-6).

He Himself bore our sins in His body on the cross, so that we might die to sin and live to righteousness; for by His wounds you were healed (1 Peter 2:24).

It can't be comforting to be wrong about the most important person in history. How can a Christian who claims to believe in Jesus Christ as his Lord and Savior continue to hold up an organization that denies the truth about Christ? Jesus Himself spoke to a similar situation: "Why do you call me 'Lord, Lord' and do not do what I say?" (Luke 6:46); and, "Not everyone who says to Me, 'Lord, Lord' will enter the kingdom of heaven; but he who does the will of my Father who is in heaven will enter" (Matthew 7:21).

MASONRY AND CHRISTIANS

37

IS THERE ANY HARMONY BETWEEN MASONRY AND CHRISTIANITY?

Masonic ritual and its solemn oaths demand that the Christian Mason's first allegiance be to Masonry. Knowingly or unknowingly, the Christian Mason participates in oaths and rituals that assist him in denying Christ. The Scriptures speak bluntly to this:

> Do not be bound together with unbelievers; for what partnership have righteousness and lawlessness, or what fellowship has light with darkness? Or what harmony has Christ with Belial [a Hebrew term for the devil], or what has a believer in common with an unbeliever? Or what agreement has the temple of God with idols?..."Therefore, come out from their midst and be separate," says the Lord (2 Corinthians 6:14-17).

We have now seen and documented—from the Lodge's own rituals and teaching authorities—Masonry's views on salvation, the Bible, God, and Jesus Christ:

- Masonry claims it offers no plan of salvation. But it actually does offer a plan of salvation through works righteousness.

- Freemasonry claims it is not a religion and even claims to support the church. But it actually is a religion in contrast to and in competition with Christianity.

- Masonry claims it respects the Bible as a Great Light. But it actually distorts the Bible and teaches that it is only a symbol of a "higher" truth, not to be obeyed literally. (In fact, the Bible may be considered of less importance than the other Masonic symbols—the Square and Compass—for in Masonry these are universal symbols throughout the earth, but the Bible is only a local symbol for Christian cultures.)

- In areas where Christianity is influential, Masonry has claimed that the God of Christianity is the God of Masonry. But this, too, is not actually the case.

- Finally, Masonry claims that it does not dishonor Jesus Christ. This also is false.

In spite of all the foregoing, Masonic ritual repeatedly tells the Christian Mason that there is nothing in the ritual or in Masonry that will interfere with his religion or with the duties he owes to his God. It states in its second degree,

> I *assure you* there is *nothing therein* [in the Entered Apprentice degree] that is incompatible with your civil or religious duties, or with those higher and nobler duties which you owe to God, your country, your neighbor, your family, or yourself. With this assurance, do you still desire to proceed? (65:39, emphasis added).

In its third degree, it declares to the candidate,

> The third degree is the cement of the whole [Blue Lodge]....
> Yet I will give it to you with the *assurance that in all its solemn words there is not one incompatible with your civil or religious duties,* or with those higher and nobler duties which you owe to God, your country, your neighbor, your

family, or yourself. With this assurance, do you still desire to proceed? (65:58, emphasis added).

In the sixth degree of the York Rite, the degree of Most Excellent Master, the initiate is told, "I assure you, as before, [this oath] is neither to affect your religion nor politics" (58:206).

Mackey's Revised Encyclopedia of Freemasonry affirms of Masonry that "there is nothing in it repugnant to the faith of a Christian" (96,II:847). Masonic authority Rev. George Oliver believes that Masonry "exists to assist or to support the church" (74:211). Leading Masonic scholar Albert Pike argued that Masonic rites and teachings "utter no word that can be deemed irreverent by anyone of any faith" (26:524). Over and over again, as the initiate progresses up the Masonic ladder, he is promised before God and men that nothing he does in Masonry will conflict with his religious beliefs.

Should not Masons delete these assurances from their ritual and writings...so that at least they would not be making promises they cannot keep?

38

IF A CHRISTIAN HAS SWORN OATHS PROMISING TO UPHOLD THE TRUTHS OF MASONRY, WHAT SHOULD HE DO?

To be a member of the Masonic Lodge, men must swear solemn oaths that place them, especially ones who are Christian, in a predicament. The oaths are frightening and are considered to be binding for one's entire life—indeed, "for all time" (73:53).

Consider the questions we once asked a Christian Mason: "As a Christian Mason, were you aware that the Masonic oaths were meant to bind you so strongly to Masonry that you would never be able to extricate yourself? Aren't you still a Mason today because of your fear of the oaths you took—even if you already know that Masonry is not Christian?"

In this section we will show Christian Masons how they can biblically deal with the oaths they swore. Many Christians are bothered by their Masonry—yet they continue to remain Masons, in part due to their oaths. A secular researcher of Masonry observed,

> It has been said that these issues [swearing the Masonic oaths] are of no concern to Freemasons, but hundreds of members of the Brotherhood have spoken to me of the turmoil they experience in attempting to reconcile their religious views with the demands of Masonic ritual....The average Christian man who has not studied the theological implications of the oaths, rituals and lectures usually experiences a certain initial moral and religious disquiet about what he has done in joining. Many have admitted to being somewhat ashamed by the initiation ceremony they have undergone (12:231,243).

What Masonry Claims About Its Oaths

The presentation volume for Masonry in the state of Virginia promises that "the penalties incurred for willful violation of your Masonic obligation will not be of a physical nature" but they are so stated "to impress upon the mind of each brother how serious a violation will be regarded by the members of the fraternity" (82, II:21). Carl Claudy, a former Grand Master of Masons in the District of Columbia, who was awarded many Masonic honors and distinctions (63:v-vii), admits in his writings that those who framed the Masonic penalties "intended to inspire terror" in the candidate. If he ever breaks the oaths, Claudy writes, the Mason should fear

> the loss of my self-respect. The self-abasement any true man feels who has broken a solemn pledge. *The wrath of a God blasphemed. The horror of a sin in which there is none greater....*These, then, are what the penalties really mean; these are the real consequences to me, if I violate my solemn obligations, these are what will be done to me if I

fail in living up, so far as I am able, to the covenants I made with my brethren (55:90, emphasis added).

The "intent to inspire terror" has apparently been used effectively. Writing in 1912, Wagner declared,

> That Masons believe that these penalties will be mercilessly inflicted upon them, should they betray its secrets, we know to be true in many cases. The convictions of those who have exposed the ritualism of the order, that they took their lives into their hands in doing so is proof. The numerous confessions made to the writer, on the part of both Masons and ex-Masons, is further proof (16:550).

In our conversations with Masons today, we have found that they, too, have fear in their hearts. Right or wrong, they fear the oaths they have taken; they fear the penalties; they fear the consequences of publicly betraying Masonic secrets. This is little wonder when Masonic leaders, such as thirty-third-degree Mason Manly Hall, speak of the severe consequences of breaking Masonic vows:

> Every Mason knows that a broken vow brings with it a terrible penalty....When a Mason swears that he will devote his life to [Masonry]...and then defiles his living temple,... he is breaking a vow which imposes not hours but ages of misery (35:68).

Further, both Hall and Albert Pike warn the Mason who breaks his vows that he, for example, "unfailingly invokes the retributive agencies of Nature" (35:42).

The Content of Masonry's Oaths

Masonry claims there is nothing in its oaths that will interfere with a person's particular religious beliefs. Further, Mackey declares that "the solemnity of an oath, is not, in itself forbidden by any Divine or human law" (96,II:723).

Here are some of the oaths all men entering the Lodge and proceeding through the different degrees must take.*

The oath for the Entered Apprentice obligations reads,

> "I, Peter Gabe, of my own free will and accord, in the presence of Almighty God, and this Worshipful Lodge, erected to Him,...most solemnly and sincerely promise and swear, that I will always hail, ever conceal, and never reveal, any of the arts, parts or points of the hidden mysteries of Ancient Free Masonry....All this I most solemnly, sincerely promise and swear, with a firm and steadfast resolution to perform the same, without any mental reservation or secret evasion of mind whatever, binding myself under no less penalty than that of having my throat cut across, my tongue torn out by its roots, and *my body buried in the rough sands of the sea*,...should I ever knowingly violate this my Entered Apprentice obligation. So help me God (58:34-35, emphasis in original).

The oath for the third (Master Mason) degree includes the following words:

> ...binding myself, under no less penalty than that of having my body severed in two, my bowels taken from thence and burned to ashes, the ashes scattered before the four winds of heaven, that no more remembrance might be had of so vile and wicked a wretch as I would be, should I ever, knowingly, violate this my Master Mason's obligation. So help me God (58:96).

The oath of the degree of Mark Master of the York Rite includes the penalty of dismemberment:

> Q. Have you a sign in this degree?
> A. I have several.

---

* To our women readers: If your husband or partner is a Mason, this is what he promised. A more extensive sampling is found in our book *The Secret Teachings of the Masonic Lodge*.

Q. Show me a sign. (Chopping off the right ear.)

Q. What is that called?
A. The dueguard.

Q. To what does it allude?
A. To the penalty of my obligation, that I should suffer my right ear to be smote off sooner than divulge any of the secrets of this degree unlawfully.

Q. Show me another sign. (Chopping off right hand.)

Q. What is that called?
A. The sign.

Q. To what does it allude?
A. To the additional portion of the penalty of my obligation, that I would sooner have my right hand stricken off as the penalty of an imposter than divulge any of the secrets of this degree unlawfully (58:179).

In the oath of the Past Master degree of the York Rite, the candidate says,

> I promise and swear, that the secrets of a brother of this Degree, delivered to me in charge as such, shall remain as secure and inviolable in my breast, as they were in his own before communicated to me, murder and treason excepted [is it permissible to cover up other crimes?], and those left to my own election (58:189).

The Mason continues by saying he is "binding myself under no less penalty than (in addition to all my former penalties) to have my tongue split from tip to root" (58:190).

Masons taking the Royal Arch degree of the York Rite promise,

> I would sooner have my skull struck off than divulge any of the secrets of this Degree unlawfully...and have my brain exposed to the scorching rays of the noonday sun (58:265); (see also 11:15; 20:46,139; 12:1; 21:50-52,56-57; 53:98, 265).

In the initiation of the thirtieth degree of the Scottish Rite, the Mason takes four more obligations. Among them are an oath taken at sword point and another taken "at the cost of the candidate's life." When he takes the third oath of the Knight Kadosh, "during the taking of this oath the Grand Provost of Justice holds the point of his sword to the heart of the candidate" (59,II:269). Later, the Thrice Puissant Grand Master says to the candidate,

> When your rashness prompted you to enter this awful Sanctuary, you were no doubt informed of the danger which threatened you, and of the trials which still await you. Swear therefore, upon your word of honor, never to reveal what you have seen or heard hitherto....Forget not that the slightest indiscretion will cost you your life. Are you still willing to proceed? (59,II:275).

Masonry teaches penalties like these are "merely symbolic," but it is a fact that no candidate entering Masonry is told during the ritual that the penalties of the oaths he is swearing to are merely symbolic. In the mind of who knows how many, there is no reason not to believe that every Masonic obligation is literally life-and-death. After all, those who violate their Masonic vows admit in their own oaths that they are worthy of death.

Masonic Oaths: Only Symbolic?

The question remains whether the penalties sworn during the oaths are "only symbolic." Candidates swear in God's name to have these penalties inflicted upon them. Masons also teach that God, not Masonry, is to take responsibility for inflicting punishment upon the violators of these oaths. In other words, rather than "Are the penalties literal or symbolic?" the more appropriate question might be "Who is the one to inflict the penalties?" Consider the following statement by Albert Mackey in his encyclopedia:

> We may say of what are called Masonic *penalties*, that they refer in no case to any kind of human punishment; that is to say, to any kind of punishment which is to be inflicted

by human hand or instrumentality. The true punishments of Freemasonry affect neither life nor limb. They are expulsion and suspension only. But those persons are wrong, be they mistaken friends or malignant enemies, who suppose or assert that there is any other sort of penalty which a Freemason recreant to his vows is subjected to by the laws of the Order, or that it is either the right or duty of any Freemason to inflict such penalty on an offending Brother. The obsecration [sacred prayer, entreaty, or oath] of a Freemason simply means that if he violates his vows or betrays his trust *he is worthy of such penalty, and that if such penalty were inflicted on him it would be just and proper.* "May I die," said the ancient, "if this be not true, or if I keep not this vow." Nor may any man put me to death, nor is any man required to put me to death, but only, if I so act, then would I be worthy of death. The ritualistic penalties of Freemasonry, supposing such to be, are in the hands not of men, but of God, *and are to be inflicted by God,* and not by men (96,II:760, first emphasis in original).

Could not the above Masonic oaths—coupled with the teaching that God Himself is to literally inflict the penalties—strike fear into the heart of the Masonic initiate? In the beginning, most Masons apparently take the oaths literally and fear literal consequences for denying them. Might this explain why so many Christian Masons have refused to deny Masonry—because they are fearful of the consequences of breaking their oaths? (Even some Masons have admitted that the Lodge could dissolve were it not for the secrecy of the organization and the fear of the penalties inflicted by the oaths—for example, 121:206. Is this any way to advance a brotherhood?)

The Consequences of Taking the Masonic Oaths

The oaths of Masonry protect, reinforce, and perpetuate the specific teachings of Masonry. One of the great problems with this for the Christian Mason is illustrated in the following verses: "The faith which you have, have as your own conviction before God. Happy is he who does not condemn himself in what he approves" (Romans 14:22). "We pray this in order that you may live a life worthy of the Lord and may please him in every way: bearing fruit in every good work, growing in the knowledge of God" (Colossians 1:10 NIV).

Much evidence can be produced to show the consequences of swearing the Masonic oaths. For example, husbands are not permitted to tell their wives of their oaths or their content. So when a husband deliberately keeps secrets from his wife in one area, may this not foster suspicion and distrust in other areas? Also, because Masonry teaches a man he must create his own temple for God to dwell within him and that a "good" Mason will spend as much time as possible at the Lodge, this may result in a significant amount of time being spent away from the family. In addition, church involvement may be reduced, which over the years may also result in family problems.

Finally, taking the oaths may lead men to trust the Lodge more than what they learn at church. Consider the experience of former Mason Jim Shaw:

> Through the years I must have heard hundreds of men say, "I don't need to go to church—the Lodge is good enough religion for me." So very many such men never attended a church, except with the Lodge once a year to hear Masonry exalted. They were trusting Lodge membership and their own "virtuous life" to assure them acceptance in the "Celestial Lodge Above" (20:77).

If the vows "morally force" a Christian Mason to uphold Masonry, this may cause him to slowly abandon his commitment to Christ, because Masonry comprises a worldview in opposition to Christianity. Masonry can only be upheld by downgrading one's Christian commitment. The end result is well illustrated by pastor and Christian spokesman John R. Rice:

In countless individual cases I have met...[Masons] insist continually that if they live up to the obligations of the lodge, or if they live moral and virtuous lives, they will get to Heaven....The lodges themselves are the most potent influence to teach people to depend upon their own righteousness and character instead of the blood of Christ....This doctrine largely neutralizes the preaching of the gospel everywhere (46:57).

Rice describes how his own father abandoned the biblical doctrines he once preached as a pastor of a Christian church—as a result of his involvement with the Lodge:

As his interest in the lodges grew, something happened to his spiritual life....He ceased preaching altogether....And his doctrine changed likewise....He said that he believed sincere heathen people who had a religion and earnestly tried to live up to their light were saved and did not need to be born again....Then his interest in missions and evangelism waned....He absorbed the lodge teaching. It led him away from the Bible, away from the ministry and soul winning, away from the church (46:59-60).

Is a Mason Bound to Keep the Oaths?

What should the Mason, and especially the Christian Mason, do who has already sworn such oaths? Is he bound to keep them if he now realizes that Masonry is wrong? Here is what the Bible advises:

If a person swears, speaking thoughtlessly with his lips to do evil or to do good, whatever it is that a man may pronounce by an oath, and he is unaware of it—when he realizes it, then he shall be guilty in any of these matters.

And it shall be, when he is guilty in any of these matters, that he shall confess that he has sinned in that thing; and he shall bring his trespass offering to the LORD for his sin which he has committed....So the priest shall make atonement on his behalf for his sin which he has committed, and it shall be forgiven him (Leviticus 5:4-6,10 NKJV).

In other words, if someone swears an oath and the implications are hidden from him, when he understands the implications and realizes he has offended God's moral law, then he is to immediately confess that he has sinned and repent. In the Old Testament a person was to go to the priest, confess, and offer a sacrifice for atonement. Today, a non-Christian may become a Christian (see our conclusion, "What Does Masonry Truly Offer?"), and then he, just like any Christian Mason may come to his own High, Priest, the Lord Jesus Christ, who has died on the cross for his sins. He should acknowledge he has sworn wrongly, and then repent of his oaths, ask for forgiveness, and acknowledge that he will obey God. The Bible promises all believers, "If we confess our sins, he is faithful and just and will forgive us our sins and purify us from all unrighteousness" (1 John 1:9 NIV).

To reinforce what we have said, when a man swears the Masonic oaths, that person has promised to uphold Masonry and all its teachings (whether he knows them or not). Swearing to uphold Masonic doctrines is unscriptural and should not be a part of the Christian's life, or the life of anyone who knows Masonic doctrines are wrong. If you need a Masonic authority to help clarify this for you, consider the words of Ake Eldberg, a minister in the Church of Sweden who is also a Freemason:

> It needs to be pointed out here that anyone who finds Masonry to be in conflict with his faith has a perfect right to leave Freemasonry and to communicate the reasons for this to others. Morally, I would say that these people are not bound by their Masonic oaths if they have encountered something ungodly or anti-Christian in their lodge; their conscience must finally judge such matters. The preeminence of a man's conscience is an important part of Masonic teaching (179).

Further, in his encyclopedia, Coil writes that, if the idea that Masonry alone will get one to heaven is "a false hope," then

Masonry should abandon that hope "and devote its attention to activities where it is sure of its ground and its authority" (95:512).

Masons might wish to ask themselves, where is Masonry's authority? In anything? Only the revealed Word of God, the Bible, can tell us the truth about God, about Jesus Christ, about ourselves, about salvation, and about life after death and how to go to heaven.

WHAT DOES MASONRY TRULY OFFER?

Given all that Masonry teaches—only some of which we have presented—is it any wonder that Lutheran pastor, former Mason, and authority on Masonry Martin Wagner concluded,

> The whole system is a giant evil. We firmly believe that it is the greatest foe that the church has to contend against. It insidiously undermines and overthrows the very foundations of evangelical Christianity. Its tendency is to make men indifferent to doctrine and hostile to the positive teachings of [the Bible] (16:24).

And it is to the Bible that we must now turn for our final statement to Masons, particularly to those who are Christian Masons.

It is revealed in the Bible that the grace of God offers all men eternal treasures which they could never earn by their own efforts, or through their own personal righteousness.

1. *Complete and absolute forgiveness of every sin*—past, present, and future:

   "In Him we have redemption through His blood, the forgiveness of our trespasses, according to the riches of His grace, which He lavished on us" (Ephesians 1:7-8).

   "He forgave us *all* our sins" (Colossians 2:13 NIV).

2. *An intimate and personal relationship with an infinitely wise, loving and holy God:*

"This is eternal life, that they may know You, the only true God, and Jesus Christ whom You have sent....The glory which You have given me I have given to them, that they may be one, just as We are one; I in them and You in me, that they may be perfected in unity, so that the world may know that You sent Me, and loved them, even as You have loved Me. Father, I desire that they also, whom You have given Me, be with Me where I am, so that they may see My glory" (John 17:3,22-24).

3. *Divine power to live a new life* that produces the fruit of the Holy Spirit: "love, joy, peace, patience, kindness, goodness, faithfulness, gentleness, self-control" (Galatians 5:22-23).

4. *A future life in heaven which will never end*—an eternal life with a perfect God, full of joy, love, learning, challenge, fellowship, wonder, glory, and worship:

"If children, heirs also, heirs of God and fellow heirs with Christ....The sufferings of this present time are not worthy to be compared with the glory that is to be revealed to us" (Romans 8:17-18).

"I saw a new heaven and a new earth; for the first heaven and the first earth passed away, and there is no longer any sea....And I heard a loud voice from the throne, saying, 'Behold, the tabernacle of God is among men, and He will dwell among them, and they shall be His people, and God Himself will be among them, and He will wipe away every tear from their eyes; and there will no longer be any death; there will no longer be any mourning, or crying, or pain; the first things have passed away.' And He who sits on the throne said, 'Behold, I am making all things new.' .And He said, 'Write, for these words are faithful and true'" (Revelation 21:1,3-5).

Indeed, the Bible teaches that every believer in Christ was saved "so that in the ages to come He [God] might show the surpassing riches of His grace and kindness towards us in Christ Jesus" (Ephesians 2:7).

Can Masonry offer any of this? Does it offer forgiveness of sins or personal fellowship with God? Does it give power to live the kind of life we know we should live? Does it give the assurance of salvation and the certain knowledge of the truth? Does it secure an eternal life in heaven with the one true God? Masonry can do none of these things—but Jesus Christ can do all of them because He is the true God, close to us all, indwelling His children.

If you are convinced you are a sinner, and that Jesus died and paid for your sins on the cross, and if you are willing to confess your sins to Him and trust Him to make you a Christian, you may do so by saying the following prayer:

> *Lord Jesus, I know now that Masonry does not bring honor to You. I confess that I am a sinner. I believe that You died for my sins on the cross. I receive You now as my Savior and ask You to give me the resolve and strength to turn from what is wrong and to live a life that is pleasing to You.*

If you prayed the above prayer or have any questions on the Christian life, write us at *The John Ankerberg Show*, P.O. Box 8977, Chattanooga TN 37414, and we will be pleased to send you some materials to help you grow as a Christian.

WHAT IS THE PROBLEM
OF MASONIC BROTHERHOOD?

If Masonry is unable even to unite its own brotherhood into harmony, how can it expect to unite the vastly competing religions of the world into a universal brotherhood?

The historic and contemporary disputes among Masons themselves make the claim that Masonry can attain a universal brotherhood impossible to justify. For example, in 1858 Albert Pike wrote about the different Masonic disputes in an article titled "The Evil Consequences of Schisms and Disputes for Power in Masonry, and of Jealousies and Dissensions Between Masonic Rites" (51,V:13). A century-and-a-half after Pike wrote that article, nothing has changed. The liberal and universal approach Masonry takes toward itself is its own worst enemy. By stressing individualism and subjectivism, Masonry ensures that it will never achieve a universal brotherhood. For example, an article in *Masonic Square* magazine from 1976 noted,

> Each Grand Lodge makes its own judgment in the light of its own approach to what Freemasonry means....So, of course, many opinions differ on what is considered basic Masonry....All this goes to demonstrate that one must be very careful before applying the practices of one Grand Lodge in the lodges of another, for they may be based on quite different esoteric [hidden] thinking to an extent

where one can be a complete contradiction of the meaning behind another. This can apply even within one jurisdiction (44,II:122-123).

Another Masonic author goes so far as to say that Masonry must change its "evil activities":

> Certain undesirable aspects of the Masonic work and organization must inevitably disappear. The appetite of the curiosity seekers, the private political machinations of certain Masonic groups, and the purely social and commercial incentives which govern much of the Masonic politics in many lands must end....Old and evil activities will come to an end....Selfishness, ambition, separativeness, wrong motives and political propaganda must fade out all together. They have no place in Masonry. They run counter to the plans of the Divine Design (40:24-25).

Referring to the "crisis" in the decline of membership in Masonry, one recent internal report noted,

> Our membership decline has two basic causes. (1) The first is that negative attitudes and practices within the ranks of past Leadership have been, too long, allowed to infect the general membership. (2) The second cause is that this Leadership has failed to ascertain and positively apply appropriate corrective changes in the outer workings of The Craft (202).

Masons are unable to agree on major issues, such as who God is (51:118; 36:192), and whether He is even relevant or not:

> British, Irish, Colonial, American, and other Grand Lodges have broken off communication and the right of inter-visitations with lodges and members of Latin Freemasonry who do not insist upon subscription to a belief in the existence of a Supreme Being and the doctrine of immortality (51,IV:258).

Further, French Masonry is, apparently, actually atheistic.

Inside the Lodge, Masons cannot even agree on minor issues. In one of the most damning indictments of Masonry's claim to brotherhood ever published, Masonic scholar Oliver Street wrote,

We read in our Monitors and in the effusions of Masonic orators of the "Universality of Masonry," and how that Masonry "unites men of every country, sect and opinion."...We stare and our bosoms heave with pride that we belong to so beneficial and so universal a brotherhood. It is a beautiful fiction which it is a pity to destroy, but the lamentable fact is there is not a word of truth in it....There is not and never has been and, if many of our most estimable brethren can have their way, there never will be universal Masonry....The Masonries which exist among many others are repudiated and denied by one another and by the Masonry of the English-speaking countries in particular....

The most trivial and absurd difference in either doctrine or practice is seized upon by some Grand Lodge, which imagines it is the conservator of pure and unadulterated Freemasonry, to erect impassible barriers between the Masonic bodies of the world. Among the most rancorous disputes that the world has ever witnessed are those that have raged among Masons during the last 200 years over questions of minor or no importance....The intolerance on the part of many Masons and Masonic bodies towards others claiming to be Masonic are so extreme that they frown even on any suggestion of getting acquainted or of even conferring together....

Self-sufficient in our own conceit, we will not admit that we can learn anything of value from the Masons of other countries and in our smug complacence we say that they are "impossible" as Masons. It is precisely the same mental attitude of Greek toward Barbarian, ancient Hebrew toward Gentile, Pharisee toward Samaritan which we so unsparingly condemn in others, but which we, like them, cannot see in ourselves....This ignorant and narrow provincialism will forever prevent the Masons of the world getting together (51,I:115-117).

In spite of all the foregoing, consider the following ideas:

- Newton believes that Masonry will result in "a great order of men, selected, initiated, sworn, and trained to make sweet reason and the will of God prevail!" (77:241).

- Former Freemason Edmond Ronayne cites McClenachan's *Book of the Ancient and Accepted Scottish Rite* as promising, "Masonry at last shall conquer, and its altar be the world" (31:111-112).

- Masonic authority Haywood believes that Masonry will bring about a new world order: "It is a world law destined to change the earth into conformity with itself, and as a world power it is something superb, awe-inspiring, godlike" (89:90).

- Albert Pike stated that the hope of the Mason is to destroy all evil in the universe and bring "the final triumph of Masonry, that shall make of all men one family and household" (51,V:35).

- *Mackey's Revised Encyclopedia of Freemasonry* argues that "the mission of Masonry is...to banish from the world every source of enmity and hostility" and to extend the principles of Masonry to all nations (96,I:269).

- Finally Newton adds that the objective of Masonry is "to bring about a universal league of mankind" (77:233).

What Is the Continuing Predicament of the Southern Baptists?

The 500,000 to 1,500,000 Masons who are also Southern Baptists present a problem for the church in general and in particular a genuine quandary for the Southern Baptists. As we noted in the introduction to this book, in 1993 the Southern Baptists issued an official report, *A Study of Freemasonry,* that concluded Lodge membership was simply a matter of individual conscience. It did not officially condemn Masonry as an anti-Christian religion that Christians should not join. Not only did this justify Lodge membership for who knows how many Christians, it also invigorated Masonry in its relationship to Christianity. Some ten years later, this conclusion still stands (185). Thus the Southern Baptists are perhaps the only conservative Christian denomination in America not to uncompromisingly warn their constituents that membership in the Masonic Lodge is not compatible with biblical teaching.

History of the Southern Baptist Report

In 1992 the Southern Baptist Convention (SBC) passed a resolution entitled "On Christian Witness and Voluntary Associations," encouraging Christians everywhere to 1) "maintain Christian witness openly before the world"; 2) avoid "any association which conflicts with clear biblical teaching" and 3) "affirm that biblical doctrine is to be open and public knowledge and that the Christian faith is to be a clear and public expression of the truth that Jesus Christ is the only means of salvation, that the Bible is our infallible guide" (199:3). Thus, the SBC effectively prohibited Christians from joining the Lodge.

Yet just a year later, the SBC reversed its position. Why?

The explanation is that thousands of Christian Masons had been actively encouraged to attend the June 1993 Southern Baptist Convention by Masonic leaders and authors, as well as by other Christian Masons. Masons realized they had much to lose at the convention vote:

> The result could be a devastating blow to Freemasonry. Minimally, it is estimated, we could lose 20% of our present members, not to mention the loss of prospective members. We should not forget that the anti-Masonic furor of 1826-56 resulted in Masonic Lodges losing as many as 75% of their members (201:10).

In our analysis, *Bowing at Strange Altars: The Masonic Lodge and the Christian Conscience*, we documented that the Masonic Lodge acknowledged it had attempted to infiltrate the Southern Baptist Convention in order to influence its vote.

The Scottish Rite Journal of February 1993 makes it clear Masonry did have an agenda to influence the vote of the Southern Baptists. This special issue was prepared, in part, in an attempt to forestall a negative conclusion at the convention. Five thousand copies of this issue were mailed to Southern Baptist leaders, and 30,000 copies were mailed to the Blue Lodges in America. Within it, the Center for Masonic Information declared it would "use radio, television, and newspapers to tell the true story of Freemasonry" (201:inside front cover). And not unexpectedly, the magazine declared that "Masonry is perfectly compatible with the classic Protestant belief in justification by faith" (201:75).

The Considerations of Other Denominations

The Southern Baptist *Study of Freemasonry* itself documents that Masonry has been rejected by the Lutheran Church—Missouri Synod, the Presbyterian Church in America, the Free Presbyterian Church of Scotland, the Greek Orthodox Church, the Church of the Nazarene, the Church of the Brethren, the Orthodox Presbyterian Church, the Assemblies of God, the Reformed Presbyterian Church; "and other Christian denominations have also taken positions against Freemasonry, or against secret societies without mentioning Freemasonry" (199).

Among the other churches or denominations that have condemned Freemasonry are the Methodist Church of England, the Wesleyan Methodist Church, the Synod Anglican Church of England, the Russian Orthodox Church, the Christian Reformed Church in America, the Roman Catholic Church, the Evangelical Mennonite Church, the Free Church of Scotland, the General Association of Regular Baptist Churches, the Church of Scotland, Grace Brethren, the Evangelical Lutheran Synod, the Independent Fundamentalist Churches of America, the Evangelical Lutheran Synod, the Baptist Union of Scotland, and the Wisconsin Evangelical Lutheran Synod.

If individual Christians can actually become Masons "in good conscience," then why all these negative conclusions condemning Masonry and urging Christians not to join the Masonic Lodge?

False Encouragement

The Southern Baptists not only failed to stand for truth, they encouraged those who stood for error. Consider this comment about the Baptist Report in the *Scottish Rite Journal* for August 1993:

> Because of your support, the vote of the Southern Baptist Convention is a historic and positive turning point for Freemasonry. Basically, it is a revitalization of our fraternity by America's largest Protestant denomination after

nearly a year of thorough, scholarly study. At the same time, it is a call to renewed effort on the part of all Freemasons today to re-energize our Fraternity and move forward to fulfilling its mission as the world's foremost proponent of the Brotherhood of Man under the Fatherhood of God.

Only God knows the full impact of this report, but we find it disheartening that the largest Protestant denomination in America has continued to fail to take any action in the ten years since its approval.

Appendix C

How Can a Mason Receive a Demit from the Masonic Lodge?

In his book, former Mason Dale Byers supplies a sample letter for Masons who desire to officially sever their ties with the Lodge. If you desire to sever your ties, we urge you to do so with a similar letter. Tell them you believe that their teaching and their vows are not biblical and that as a Christian, you can no longer participate, according to 2 Corinthians 6:14-18 and Ephesians 5:8-17. In addition, request that the letter be read to all members of your lodge in conjunction with the rules and regulations of the order. If the letter is written as described below, then Masonic law dictates that it must be read before the lodge membership. In this way your letter will be a testimony to others in the Lodge concerning the love and truth of Jesus Christ.

The letterhead and envelope must both be addressed to *the members of the Lodge*. Do not address your letter to the Lodge Master or simply to, for example, "Lodge 118," because this refers to the officers, and they will merely process the request but not read it to the members. The letter itself must begin with the salutation "To the members of Lodge number _____"—not to any particular person, only Lodge members.

Sample Letter for Receiving a Demit (125:125-126)

> To my friends and acquaintances in the Masonic Lodge:
> This letter is a formal request for my demit from the Masonic Lodge. Please remove my name from your membership rolls and mail to me a copy of my demit.

Thank you for allowing me an opportunity to express my reasons for withdrawing from the Lodge. Do understand that my withdrawal has no personal bearing upon individual members or any personal conflicts with members. Those in the Lodge who are my friends know that I still treasure their personal friendships.

However, I am a Christian and must forsake the Lodge because its teachings are contrary to the true teachings of the Bible. Freemasonry rejects the Lord Jesus Christ Who is the Lord and Master of my life. I cannot with a clear conscience be a Mason because Jesus Christ is not allowed to be named or worshiped in the Lodge as it might offend another Mason. Masonry's respected authors, Albert Mackey and Albert Pike, openly claim that Masonry is a religion. They are right! It is a religion without Christ.

Many of us have heard that the Lodge is based on the Bible. However, in Freemasonry the Bible is rejected and God's Word is misused and misquoted. The Lodge's religion is universalism and the Bible is nothing more than a symbol.

Masonry promises to its members the blessings of heaven and acceptance before God. [But] the Masonic plan of salvation is totally contrary to what the Bible teaches. Man cannot be saved apart from Jesus Christ as Savior.

In closing, may I express my love for you as individuals, and if you desire, I will gladly share how I became a Christian and help you understand how you, too, may become a follower of Jesus Christ.

Your friend in Christ,

[signature]

APPENDIX D

HOW WILL MASONS RESPOND TO THIS BOOK?

There are a number of responses that individual Masons may have to the content of this book. Some may say, "This is not what the Lodge officially teaches." Others may say, "These teachings are not consistent with what I have gathered from my years in the Lodge." Still others may say of the Masonic authorities we cite, "This is just their opinion; it has no binding authority for Masons." Others yet may say, "This is not what the men in our lodge believe." Let us answer each of these objections in turn.

1. For those who say, "This is not what the Lodge officially teaches," such persons need to recognize that their response could be sincerely wrong. The only way to find out the true case is to consult what the Masonic ritual and the accepted Masonic authorities state and teach. And it is these we have quoted.

2. Masons may claim, "This is not what I have gathered from my years of experience in the Lodge." But the fact remains that, for whatever reason, they may never have correctly understood the teachings of the Lodge. Again, the only way to find out is to consult what the ritual and the accepted authorities actually teach.

3. A common response concerning the citing of important Masonic leaders (particularly at point of tension) is that these citations are "just their opinion"—as if they had

little authority. The problem is that these men (such as Mackey, Pike, Coil, Newton, Hall, Roberts, and others) are accepted as authorities by Masonry itself, and their words are not treated as extraneous opinions. Indeed, Albert Pike was the very architect of the Scottish Rite itself—"the Master Builder of the Scottish Rite," in the words of Sovereign Grand Commander of the Scottish Rite, C. Fred Kleinknecht—so his writings can hardly just be dismissed (186:23). These men are legitimate authorities of Masonry, and their arguments cannot be dismissed because they are inconvenient or embarrassing at certain points.

4. For those who say, "This is not what the men in our lodge believe," in some cases this could be true. Such men may be out of step with the true teachings of their lodge. Christian Masons, for example, tend to interpret the ritual and teachings of the Lodge through Christian eyes. In other words, they see Christian teachings in Masonry that are not really there.

The issue at hand is whether a person is acting consistently with his professed faith. In other words, religions such as Mormonism or Jehovah's Witnesses may sound Christian, but the evidence from their own authoritative literature proves they are not. Someone could belong to a Mormon temple or a Kingdom Hall or even a Buddhist shrine and still attempt to practice Christianity. But can they do this in good conscience if they must continually compromise their Christian faith in order to hold to the practices and beliefs of the other religion? It is obviously inconsistent for a true Christian to support, believe, and practice another religion that is totally different from and actually opposed to Christianity—like Mormonism, Jehovah's Witnesses, and Buddhism—or in this case, Masonry.

ADDITIONAL RESOURCES

Recommended Reading

Stephen Tsoukalas, *Masonic Rites and Wrongs: An Examination of Freemasonry,* Phillipsburg, NJ: P&R Press, 1995.

John Ankerberg and John Weldon, *Bowing at Strange Altars: The Masonic Lodge and the Christian Conscience,* Ankerberg Theological Research Institute, 1993.

John Ankerberg and John Weldon, *The Secret Teachings of the Masonic Lodge,* Chicago: Moody Press, 1990.

Paul A. Fisher, *Behind the Lodge Door: Church, State & Freemasonry,* Washington, DC: Shield Press, 1987.

Dale A. Byers, *I Left the Lodge,* Schaumburg, IL: Regular Baptist Press, 1988.

Stephen Knight, *The Brotherhood: The Explosive Exposé of the Secret World of the Freemasons,* London, UK: Grenada Publishing, Ltd./Panther Books, 1983.

Masonic Books and Web sites

Rex R. Hutchens, *A Bridge to Light,* Washington, DC: The Supreme Council, 33rd Degree, Ancient and Accepted Scottish Rite of Freemasonry, Southern Jurisdiction, United States of America, 1988.

"Index of Webpages you can find on Paul M. Bessel's Website," Paul M. Bessel's Web site (bessel.org/webindex.htm) [Bessel is an authority for the Grand Lodge of DC in Washington, DC, and Executive Secretary of the Masonic Leadership Center].

Anti-Masonry Point of View (www.masonicinfo.com).

E-M@son Links (www.freemasonry.org/links/).

Masons.start4all.com (www.masons.start4all.com).

BIBLIOGRAPHY

Note to the Reader: Starred texts are recommended reading. Texts containing Masonic ritual or instruction are identified by "B" (Blue Lodge); "S" (Scottish Rite), or "Y" (York Rite). "MW" indicates a Masonic Web site. Texts labeled "MR" document the relation of Masonry to ancient pagan mystery religion. The number reference system is explained in the footnote on page 9.

* 1. "Christianity and the Masonic Lodge: Are They Compatible?" Transcript from *The John Ankerberg Show* (guests: William Mankin, Dr. Walter Martin), Chattanooga, TN: The John Ankerberg Evangelistic Association, 1985.

2. L. James Rongstad, *How to Respond to the Lodge*, St. Louis: Concordia, 1977.

3. The John Ankerberg Evangelistic Association, "Freemasonry on Its Own Terms," *News & Views*, May 1986, Chattanooga, TN: The John Ankerberg Evangelistic Association.

4. The John Ankerberg Evangelistic Association, *Is Freemasonry a Religion? and Other Important Questions About "The Lodge,"* Chattanooga, TN: The John Ankerberg Evangelistic Association, 1986.

5. "The Bible and Freemasonry," in *Holy Bible—Masonic Edition*, Terminal House, Shepperton, London: A. Lewis (Masonic Publishers) Ltd., 1975.

6. "Freemasonry," *Encyclopedia Britannica Micropedia*, vol. 4.

7. Paul Tschackert, "Freemasons," *The New Schaff-Herzog Encyclopedia of Religious Knowledge*, vol. 4, Grand Rapids, MI, Baker, 1977.

8. E.L. Hawkins, "Freemasonry," in James Hastings, ed., *Encyclopedia of Religion and Ethics*, vol. 6, New York: Charles Scribner's Sons, n.d.

9. The John Ankerberg Evangelistic Association, "Christianity and Freemasonry," *News & Views*, November 1987, Chattanooga, TN: The John Ankerberg Evangelistic Association.

10. E.M. Storms, *Should a Christian Be a Mason?*, Route 1, Lytle Road, Fletcher, NC: New Puritan Library, 1980.

*   11. Committee on Secret Societies of the Ninth General Assembly of the Orthodox Presbyterian Church (meeting at Rochester, NY, June 2-5, 1942), *Christ or the Lodge?*, Philadelphia, PA: Great Commission Publications, n.d.

*   12. Stephen Knight, *The Brotherhood: The Explosive Exposé of the Secret World of the Freemasons*, London, UK: Grenada Publishing, Ltd./Panther Books, 1983.

*   13. "The Masonic Lodge: What Goes on Behind Closed Doors?" Transcript from *The John Ankerberg Show* (guests: Jack Harris, William Mankin, Dr. Walter Martin, Paul Pantzer), Chattanooga, TN: The John Ankerberg Evangelistic Association, 1986.

     14. William H. Russell, *Masonic Facts for Masons*, Chicago, IL: Charles T. Powner Co., 1968.

*   15. Shildes Johnson, *Is Masonry a Religion?*, Oakland, NJ: Institute for Contemporary Christianity, 1978.

* MR16. Martin L. Wagner, *Freemasonry: An Interpretation*, n.p., n.d. (distributed by Missionary Service and Supply, Route 2, Columbiana, OH, 44408).

MR   17. W.L. Wilmshurst, *The Meaning of Masonry*, New York: Bell Publishing Co., 1980.

     18. Joseph Fort Newton, *The Religion of Masonry: An Interpretation*, Richmond, VA: Macoy Publishing and Masonic Supply Co., Inc., 1969.

*   19. J.W. Acker, *Strange Altars: A Scriptural Appraisal of the Lodge*, St. Louis, MO: Concordia, 1959.

     20. Jim Shaw and Tom McKenney, *The Deadly Deception: Freemasonry Exposed by One of Its Top Leaders*, Lafayette, LA: Huntington House, 1988.

     21. Jack Harris, *Freemasonry: The Invisible Cult in Our Midst*, Chattanooga, TN: Global, 1983.

     22. "Anglican Synod Condemns Freemasonry," *Los Angeles Times*, July 14, 1987.

     23. W.J. McCormick, *Christ, the Christian, and Freemasonry*, 1984 rev. ed., Belfast, Ireland: Great Joy Publications (USA distributors: Saints Alive in Jesus, Issaquah, WA).

     24. Kenneth W. Kemp, "What Christians Should Think About Creation Science," *Perspectives on Science and Christian Faith*, December 1988.

     25. Arthur Edward Waite, *A New Encyclopedia of Freemasonry*, combined ed., New York: Weather Vane Books, 1970.

MR   26. Albert Pike, *Morals and Dogma of the Ancient and Accepted Scottish Rite of Freemasonry*, Charleston, SC: The Supreme Council of the 33rd Degree for the Southern Jurisdiction of the United States, 1906.

27. Isabel Cooper-Oakley, *Masonry and Medieval Mysticism: Traces of a Hidden Tradition*, Wheaton, IL: Theosophical Publishing House, 1977.

28. Corinne Heline, *Mystic Masonry and the Bible*, La Canada, CA: New Age Press, 1975.

* 29. Alva J. McClain, *Freemasonry and Christianity*, Winona Lake, IN: BMH Books, 1977.

B 30. Edmond Ronayne, *Ronayne's Handbook of Freemasonry with Appendix (Mah-hah-bone)*, Chicago: Ezra A. Cook, 1976.

MR 31. Edmond Ronayne, *The Master's Carpet; or Masonry and Baal-Worship—Identical*, n.p., n.d. (distributed by Missionary Service and Supply, Route 2, Columbiana, OH 44408).

32. Booklist for A. Lewis, Ltd. (Masonic Publishers), Terminal House, Middlesex, England, January 1979.

33. Osborne Sheppard, compiler and publisher, *Freemasonry in Canada with a Concise History of Old British Lodges, the Introduction of Freemasonry into the United States of America and Other Valuable and Instructive Information*, Hamilton, Ontario: Osborne Sheppard, 1915.

34. W.J. Morris, *Pocket Lexicon of Freemasonry*, Chicago: Ezra A. Cook Publications, n.d.

MR 35. Manly P. Hall, *The Lost Keys of Freemasonry or the Secret of Hiram Abiff*, Richmond, VA: Macoy Publishing and Masonic Supply Co., Inc., 1976.

36. Henry Wilson Coil, *A Comprehensive View of Freemasonry*, Richmond, VA: Macoy Publishing and Masonic Supply Co., 1973.

37. Stephen R. Sywulka, "The Pope Uses Masonic Scandal to Stiffen Traditional Stance," *Christianity Today*, June 26, 1981.

38. F. De P. Castells, *The Genuine Secrets in Freemasonry Prior to A.D. 1717*, London, England: A. Lewis, 1971.

39. Edmond Ronayne, *Freemasonry at a Glance*, Chicago, IL: Ezra A. Cook Publications, 1904.

MR 40. Foster Bailey, *The Spirit of Masonry*, Hampstead, London: Lucius Press, Ltd., 1972.

41. Harold Waldwin Percival, *Masonry and Its Symbols in the Light of "Thinking and Destiny,"* Forest Hills, NY: The Word Foundation, Inc., 1979.

42. Douglas Knoop, G.P. Jones, and Douglas Hamer, transcribers and eds., *The Early Masonic Catechisms*, London, England: Quatuor Coronati Lodge No. 2076, London, 1975.

43. George H. Steinmetz, *Freemasonry—Its Hidden Meaning*, Chicago: Charles T. Powner Co., 1976.

44. *Masonic Square for 1975 and 1976* (bound volume), vol. 1: March 1975–December 1975; vol. 2: March 1976–December 1976.

Y   45. John Sheville and James Gould, *Guide to the Royal Arch Chapter: A Complete Monitor with Full Instructions in the Degrees of Mark Master, Past Master, Most Excellent Master and Royal Arch Together With the Order of High Priesthood*, Richmond, VA: Macoy Publishing and Masonic Supply Co., 1981.

46. John R. Rice, *Lodges Examined by the Bible*, Murfreesboro, TN: Sword of the Lord Publishers, 1943.

48. Kent Henderson, *Masonic World Guide*, Richmond, VA: Macoy Publishing and Masonic Supply Co., 1984.

49. H.V.B. Voorhis, *Facts for Freemasons: A Storehouse of Masonic Knowledge in Question and Answer Form*, rev. ed., Richmond, VA: Macoy Publishing and Masonic Supply, 1979.

50. Rollin C. Blackmer, *The Lodge and the Craft*, Richmond, VA: Macoy Publishing and Masonic Supply, 1976.

51. Various authors, *Little Masonic Library* (5 volumes), Richmond, VA: Macoy Publishing and Masonic Supply, 1977.

S   52. The Ancient and Accepted Scottish Rite of Freemasonry, Southern Jurisdiction USA, *Ceremonies of Installation and Dedication*, 1954 rev.

Y   53. The General Grand Chapter of Royal Arch Masons International, Committee on Revision of the Ritual (William F. Kuhn, et al.) *The Manual of Ritual for Royal Arch Masons*, 45th ed., 1983.

B   54. George Simmons and Robert Macoy, *Standard Masonic Monitor of the Degrees of Entered Apprentice, Fellow Craft and Master Mason*, Richmond, VA: Macoy Publishing and Masonic Supply, 1984.

55. Carl H. Claudy, *Foreign Countries: A Gateway to the Interpretation and Development of Certain Symbols of Freemasonry*, Richmond, VA: Macoy Publishing and Masonic Supply, 1971.

56. James Royal Case, *The Case Collection: Biographies of Masonic Notables*, The Missouri Lodge of Research, 1984.

MR   57. Alphonse Cerza, *A Masonic Reader's Guide*, Thomas C. Warden, ed., Transactions of the Missouri Lodge of Research, vol. 34 (1978–1979), 1980.

B,Y 58. Malcolm C. Duncan, *Masonic Ritual and Monitor*, New York: David McKay Co., n.d.

S   59. John Blanchard, *Scottish Rite Masonry Illustrated: The Complete Ritual of the Ancient and Accepted Scottish Rite* (two volumes), Chicago: Charles T. Powner Co., 1979. For evidence documenting the accuracy and authority of this book, see 174:65-67 and pp. 46-51. The publisher states, "To the best of our knowledge, the book 'Scottish Rite Masonry Illustrated' is accurate and current. This book is one of our best sellers and is sold throughout the United States. Both Lodges and Masonic bookstores buy this book in large quantities. We have never had any complaints regarding the accuracy of the above titled book" (M. Bytnar, Vice-President, Charles T. Powner Company, letter to Dr. Weldon, April 6, 1993, on file.)

60. Carl H. Claudy, *Introduction to Freemasonry* (three volumes), Washington, DC: The Temple Publishers, 1984.

Y 61. Ezra A. Cook Publications, *Revised Knight Templarism Illustrated*, Chicago: Ezra A. Cook, 1986.

B 62. The Free and Accepted Masons of Arkansas, Grand Lodge, *Masonic Monitor of the Degrees of Entered Apprentice, Fellow Craft and Master Mason*, 7th ed., Free and Accepted Masons of Arkansas, 1983.

63. Carl H. Claudy, *The Master's Book*, Washington, DC: The Temple Publishers, 1985.

B 64. Harris Bullock et al., *Masonic Manual of the Grand Lodge of Georgia, Free and Accepted Masons*, The Grand Lodge of Georgia, 1983.

B 65. Raymond Lee Allen et al., *Tennessee Craftsmen or Masonic Textbook*, 14th ed., Nashville, TN: Tennessee Board of Custodians Members, 1963.

B 66. William W. Daniel et al., *Masonic Manual of the Grand Lodge of Georgia*, 9th ed. *Free and Accepted Masons*, Grand Lodge of Georgia, 1973.

B 67. Ezra A. Cook Publications, *Blue Lodge Enlight'ment: A Ritual of the Three Masonic Degrees*, Chicago: Ezra A. Cook, 1964.

Y 68. E. Ronayne, *Chapter Masonry*, Chicago: Ezra A. Cook, 1984.

B 69. Grand Lodge of Texas, A.F. and A.M., *Monitor of the Lodge: Monitorial Instructions in the Three Degrees of Symbolic Masonry*, Grand Lodge of Texas, 1982.

70. Henry Wilson Coil, *Freemasonry Through Six Centuries* (two volumes), Richmond, VA: Macoy Publishing and Masonic Supply, 1967.

71. Awad Khoury, tr., *The Origin of Masonry*, n.p., n.d. (originally pub. 1897).

72. H.J. Rogers, *The Word of God vs. Masonry*, Van Alstyne, TX: B & R Publishers, n.d.

* 73. Alphonse Cerza, *Let There Be Light: A Study in Anti-Masonry*, Silver Spring, MD: The Masonic Service Association, 1983.

74. H.L. Haywood, *The Newly-Made Mason: What He and Every Mason Should Know About Masonry*, Richmond, VA: Macoy Publishing and Masonic Supply, 1973.

75. Nobles of the Mystic Shrine, *Proceedings of the 90th Annual Session—Imperial Council of the Ancient Arabic Order of the Nobles of the Mystic Shrine for North America* (Iowa Corporation), New York: 1964.

76. Allen E. Roberts, *Key to Freemasonry's Growth*, Richmond, VA: Macoy Publishing and Masonic Supply, 1969.

77. Joseph Fort Newton, *The Builders: A Story and Study of Freemasonry*, Richmond, VA: Macoy Publishing and Masonic Supply, 1951.

78. John H. Van Gorden, ed., *Masonic Charities*, Lexington, MA: The Supreme Council, 33rd Degree, Ancient Accepted Scottish Rite of Freemasonry; Northern Masonic Jurisdiction, USA, 1987.

79. Allen E. Roberts, *The Craft and Its Symbols: Opening the Door to Masonic Symbolism*, Richmond, VA: Macoy Publishing and Masonic Supply, 1974.

80. Henry C. Clausen, *Beyond the Ordinary: Toward a Better, Wiser and Happier World*, Washington, DC: The Supreme Council, 33rd Degree, Ancient and Accepted Scottish Rite of Freemasonry, 1983.

81. Holy Bible (Temple Illustrated Edition), Nashville, TN: A.J. Holman Co., 1968.

B   82. John Dove, compiler, *Virginia Textbook (Containing "The Book of Constitutions," Illustrations of the Work, Forms and Ceremonies of the Grand Lodge of Virginia*, Grand Lodge of Virginia, n.d.

S   83. Southern Jurisdiction of the United States of America, *Funeral Ceremony and Offices of a Lodge of Sorrow of the Ancient and Accepted Scottish Rite of Freemasonry*, Charleston, SC: 1946, rpt.

S   84. Southern Jurisdiction of the USA, *Ceremonies of Installation and Dedication...of the Ancient and Accepted Scottish Rite of Freemasonry*, The Ancient and Accepted Scottish Rite of Freemasonry, Southern Jurisdiction, USA, 1954.

85. Henry G. Meacham, *Our Stations and Places*, New York: Grand Lodge, F. and A.M. Committee on Lodge Sales, 1967.

86. Holy Bible—Masonic Edition, Philadelphia, PA: A.J. Holman, 1939.

87. Arthur Herrmann, *Designs upon the Trestleboard: A Guidebook for Masters and Wardens*, Richmond, VA: Macoy Publishing and Masonic Supply, 1980.

88. William J. Hughan et al., *Freemasonry*, Washington, DC: Library of the Supreme Council, 33rd Degree, 1958 (rpt. from the *Encyclopedia Britannica*).

89. H.L. Haywood, *The Great Teachings of Masonry*, Richmond, VA: Macoy Publishing and Masonic Supply, 1971.

MR 90. Albert G. Mackey, *The Symbolism of Freemasonry: Illustrating and Explaining Its Science and Philosophy, Its Legends, Myths, and Symbols*, Chicago: Charles T. Powner Co., 1975.

S   91. Henry C. Clausen, *Practice and Procedure for the Scottish Rite*, Washington, DC: The Supreme Council, 33rd Degree, Ancient and Accepted Scottish Rite of Freemasonry Mother Jurisdiction of the World, 1981.

92. Educational and Historical Commission of the Grand Lodge of Georgia, *Leaves from Georgia Masonry*, Educational and Historical Commission of the Grand Lodge of Georgia, 1947.

S 93. Albert Pike, *Liturgy of the Ancient and Accepted Scottish Rite of Freemasonry for the Southern Jurisdiction of the United States, Part Two*, Washington, DC: The Supreme Council, 33rd Degree of the Ancient and Accepted Scottish Rite of Freemasonry of the Southern Jurisdiction of the USA, 1982.

94. Henry C. Clausen, *Clausen's Commentaries on Morals and Dogma*, The Supreme Council, 33rd Degree, Ancient and Accepted Scottish Rite of Freemasonry, Southern Jurisdiction of the USA, 1976.

95. Henry Wilson Coil, *Coil's Masonic Encyclopedia*, New York: Macoy Publishing and Masonic Supply, 1961.

MR 96. Albert G. Mackey, *Mackey's Revised Encyclopedia of Freemasonry* (revised and enlarged by Robert I. Clegg) (three volumes), Richmond, VA: Macoy Publishing and Masonic Supply, 1966.

97. William C. Irvine, *Heresies Exposed*, Neptune, NJ: Loizeaux Brothers, 1970.

98. "Freemasonry," in Richard Cavendish, ed., *Man, Myth and Magic: An Illustrated Encyclopedia of the Supernatural*, New York: Marshall Cavendish Corporation, 1970.

99a. Legenda 32 (Part 1). This is a Masonic source apparently used for instruction, circa 1920–1930. No publisher, author, or date is given.

99b. Legenda, *Scottish Rite*, XIX to XXX, 26th degree (Part 2).

B 100. Henry Pirtle, *Kentucky Monitor: Complete Monitorial Ceremonies of the Blue Lodge*, Louisville, KY: Standard Printing Co., 1921.

101. Editorial by Francis G. Paul, "The Test Never Changes," *The Northern Light: A Window for Freemasonry*, May 1988.

102. The Working Group established by the Standing Committee of the General Synod of the Church of England, *Freemasonry and Christianity: Are They Compatible?*, London: Church House Publishing, 1987.

103. The Baptist Union of Scotland (endorsed by the Baptist Union of Great Britain and Ireland), *Baptists and Freemasonry*, Baptist Church House, 1987.

104. Report of the Faith and Order Committee of the British Methodist Church, *Freemasonry and Methodism*, 1985. (Presented to the General Assembly of the British Methodist Church and adopted by them Wednesday, July 3, 1985.)

105. Albert Mackey, *The Manual of the Lodge*, New York: Clark Maynard, 1870.

106. *Webster's New World Dictionary*, second collegiate ed., New York: Simon & Schuster, 1984.

107. *Oxford American Dictionary*, New York: Avon, 1982.

108. *Webster's New Twentieth Century Dictionary*, second ed. unabridged, Collins–World, 1978.

109. See C.S. Lewis, *Mere Christianity*, (Macmillan); Henry M. Morris, *Many Infallible Proofs* (Master Books); and Os Guinness, *In Two Minds* (Inter-Varsity).

*   110. "Checking It Out" (Masonic Affiliates), *News & Views*, August 1986, Chattanooga, TN: The John Ankerberg Evangelistic Association.

111. A.E. Cundall, "Baal," in Merrill C. Tenney, ed., *The Zondervan Pictorial Encyclopedia of the Bible*, vol. 1, Grand Rapids, MI: Zondervan, 1975.

112. "Baal," in *Encyclopedia Britannica—Micropedia*, vol. 1, Chicago: University of Chicago, 1978.

113. "Baal," in *The New Schaff-Herzog Encyclopedia of Religious Knowledge*, vol. 1, Grand Rapids, MI: Baker, 1977.

114. Lewis Bayles Payton, "Baal, Beel, Bel," in James Hastings, ed., *Encyclopedia of Religion and Ethics*, vol. 2, New York, Charles Scribner's Sons, n.d.

115. George A. Barton, "Baalzebub and Beelzaboul" in reference 114.

116. W.L. Liefeld, "Mystery Religions," in Merrill C. Tenney, ed., *The Zondervan Pictorial Encyclopedia of the Bible*, vol. 4, Grand Rapids, MI: Zondervan, 1977.

116a. John Gray, "Baal—The Dying and Rising God," in Richard Cavendish, ed., *Man, Myth and Magic: An Illustrated Encyclopedia of the Supernatural*, vol. 2, New York: Marshall Cavendish Corp., 1970.

117. Congressional Record, Senate, September 9, 1987, pp. S11868-70.

MR 118. Manly Hall, *An Encyclopedic Outline of Masonic, Hermetic, Qabbalistic and Rosicrucian Symbolical Philosophy*, Los Angeles Philosophical Research Society, 1977.

119. Arthur Avalon, *The Serpent Power*, New York: Dover, 1974; Gopi Krishna, *The Awakening of Kundalini*, New York: Dutton, 1975; Hans-Ulrich Rieker, *The Yoga of Light*, Los Angeles: Dawn Horse, 1974.

120. Charles H. Lacquement, "Freemasonry and Organized Religions," *The Pennsylvania Freemason*, February 1989.

*   121. Paul A. Fisher, *Behind the Lodge Door: Church, State & Freemasonry*, Washington, DC: Shield Press, 1987.

122. Captain William Morgan, *Illustrations of Masonry by One of the Fraternity*, 1827, n.p.

123. Charles G. Finney, *The Character, Claims and Practical Workings of Freemasonry*, Southern District of Ohio, Western Tract and Book Society, 1869.

124. C.F. McQuaig, *The Masonic Report*, Columbiana, OH: Missionary Service and Supply, 1976.

125. Dale A. Byers, *I Left the Lodge*, Schaumburg, IL: Regular Baptist Press, 1988.

126. "Mystery Religions," *Encyclopedia Britannica Macropedia*, vol. 12, pp. 778-85.

127. G.W. Gilmore, "Tribal and Cultic Mysteries," in *The New Schaff-Herzog Encyclopedia of Religious Knowledge*, Grand Rapids, MI: Baker Books, 1977.

128. P. Gardner, "Mysteries," in James Hastings, ed., *Encyclopedia of Religion and Ethics*, vol. 9, New York: Charles Scribner's Sons, n.d.

129. Paul Lee Tan, *Encyclopedia of 7700 Illustrations*, Rockville, MD: Assurance, 1979.

130. Frits Staal, *Exploring Mysticism*, Berkeley, CA: University of California Press, 1975; Benjamin B. Wolman, Montague Ullman, eds., *Handbook of States of Consciousness*, New York: Van Nostrand Reinhold, 1986.

131. John Ferguson, *An Illustrated Encyclopedia of Mysticism and the Mystery Religions*, New York: Seabury Press, 1977; cf. reference 130, Wolman, ed., pp. 286-90.

132. E.g., John Ankerberg and John Weldon, *The Facts on Spirit Guides; The Facts on the New Age Movement; The Facts on Astrology*, all Eugene, OR: Harvest House, 1988.

133. See reference 132; Paul and Teri Reisser and John Weldon, *New Age Medicine*, Downers Grove, IL: InterVarsity, 1988, ch. 6; Ben Hester, *Dowsing: An Exposé of Hidden Occult Forces* (write the author: 4883 Hedrick Avenue, Arlington, CA 92505); Clifford Wilson and John Weldon, *Psychic Forces*, Chattanooga, TN: Global, 1988, pp. 331-445; John Weldon and James Bjornstad, *Playing With Fire: Dungeons and Dragons and Other Fantasy Games*, Chicago: Moody, 1984, ch. 5; John Weldon and Zola Levitt, *Psychic Healing*, Chicago: Moody Press, 1982, ch. 3 ("Radionics"); Edmund Gruss, *The Ouija Board*, Chicago: Moody Press, 1975.

134. C.F. Keil and F. Delitzsch, *Commentary on the Old Testament in Ten Volumes*, Grand Rapids, MI: Eerdmans, 1978.

* 135. John Ankerberg, and John Weldon, *The Facts on the Masonic Lodge*, Eugene, OR: Harvest House, 1989.

* 136. John Ankerberg and John Weldon, *Christianity and the Secret Teachings of the Masonic Lodge: What Goes on Behind Closed Doors?*, Chattanooga, TN: John Ankerberg Evangelistic Association, 1989.

137. E.K. Simpson and F.F. Bruce, *Commentary on the Epistles to the Ephesians and Colossians*, Grand Rapids, MI: Wm. B. Eerdmans, 1975.

138. Alexander Solzhenitsyn, *Warning to the West*, New York: Farrar, Straus and Giroux, 1977.

139. *The Iowa Quarterly Bulletin*, April 1917.

140. Donald Barnhouse, *Genesis: A Devotional Exposition*, vol. 1, Grand Rapids, MI: Zondervan, 1970.

141. Leon Morris, *Christianity Today*, March 4, 1977.

142. Lewis Sperry Chafer, *Major Bible Themes*, Grand Rapids, MI: Zondervan, 1926.

143. Lewis Sperry Chafer, *Systematic Theology*, vol. 4, Dallas, TX: Dallas Seminary Press, 1971.

144. Harold O.J. Brown, *The Protest of a Troubled Protestant*, New Rochelle, NY: Arlington House, 1969.

145. C.S. Lewis, *The Great Divorce*, New York: Macmillan, 1946.

146. C.S. Lewis, *The Problem of Pain*, New York: Macmillan, 1971.

147. M. Scott Peck, *People of the Lie*, New York: Simon & Schuster, 1981.

148. *Chalcedon Report*, January 1984, Box 158, Vallecito, CA.

149. Cited in *Eternity* magazine, October 1985.

150. Alice A. Bailey, *The Externalization of the Hierarchy*, New York: Lucis Publishing Co., 1948.

151. *The Bulletin of the Atomic Scientists*, June 1976.

152. *The Stockton* (California) *Herald*, for the week of March 13-18, 1960, or March 3-8, 1963.

153. Albert Mackey, *Mackey's Masonic Ritualist: Monitorial Instructions and the Degrees from Entered Apprentice to Select Masters*, Charles E. Merrill Co., 1867.

154. John C. Green, *The Death of Adam: Evolution and Its Impact on Western Thought*, Iowa State University Press, 1959.

155. Cited in David Lack, *Evolutionary Theory and Christian Belief*, London, UK: Methuen, 1957.

156. John Ankerberg and John Weldon, *Astrology: Does It Determine Your Destiny?* Eugene, OR: Harvest House, 1989, chaps. 14-15.

157. J.I. Packer, *God's Words: Studies of Key Bible Themes*, Downers Grove, IL: InterVarsity, 1981.

158. Antony Flew and Alasdair MacIntyre, eds., "Theology and Falsification" in *New Essays in Philosophical Theology*, London, UK: SCM Press, 1955.

159. Merrill F. Unger, *Archeology and the Old Testament*, Grand Rapids, MI: Zondervan, 1977.

160. Lawrence E. Stager and Samuel R. Wolf, "Child Sacrifice at Carthage [and in the Bible]: Religious Rite or Population Control?" *Biblical Archeology Review*, January–February 1984.

161. *Webster's Collegiate Dictionary*, fifth ed., Springfield, MA: G & C Merriam & Co., 1946.

162. Amihai Mazar, "Bronze Bull Found in Israelite 'High Place' from the Time of the Judges," *Biblical Archeology Review*, September–October, 1983.

163. William Lane Craig, *The Son Rises*, Chicago: Moody Press, 1981; Frank Morison, *Who Moved the Stone?*, Downers Grove, IL: InterVarsity, 1969; Gary Habermas and Antony Flew, *Did Jesus Rise From the Dead? The Resurrection Debate*, San Francisco: Harper & Row, 1987.

164. Jim Tresner, "Conscience and the Craft," *The Scottish Rite Journal*, February 1993, emphasis added; cf. J.N.D. Anderson, *Christianity and Comparative Religion*, Downers Grove, IL: InterVarsity Press, 1977, pp.11-12.

165. "A Response to Critics of Freemasonry," The Masonic Information Center (8120 Fenton St., Silver Spring, MD 20910-4785; 301-588-4010 or fax 301-608-3457).

* 166. Eddy D. Field II and Eddy D. Field III, "Freemasonry and the Christian," *The Master's Seminary Journal*, Fall 1994, 141–57 (http://www.tms.edu/tmsj/tmsj5g.pdf).

MW167. "Freemasonry Primer." Anti-Masonry Points of View Web site (www.masonicinfo.com/primer.htm.)

* 168. Steven Tsoukalas, *Masonic Rites and Wrongs: An Examination of Freemasonry*, Phillipsburg, NJ: P&R Press, 1995.

MW169. "Anti-Masonry Examined," Ake Eldberg's home page Web site. (http://home.swipnet.se/~w-49954/Antimas/).

MW170. Trevor W. McKeown, "Anti-masonry—Frequently Asked Questions," Grand Lodge of British Columbia and Yukon Web site (freemasonry.bcy.ca/anti-masonry/anti-masonry_faq.html).

MW171. "Anti-masonic claims refuted," Grand Lodge of British Columbia and Yukon Web site (freemasonry.bcy.ca/anti-masonry/index.html).

172. John Ankerberg and John Weldon, *The Secret Teachings of the Masonic Lodge*, Chicago: Moody Press, 1990.

173. Albert G. Mackey, *An Encyclopedia of Freemasonry and Its Kindred Sciences*, vol. 1, Chicago: Masonic History Company, 1921.

174. John Ankerberg and John Weldon, *Bowing at Strange Altars: The Masonic Lodge and the Christian Conscience*, Chattanooga, TN: Ankerberg Theological Research Institute, 1993.

175. Sovereign Grand Commander of the Scottish Rite C. Fred Kleinknecht said of Pike, "He will always be remembered and revered as the Master Builder of the Scottish Rite" (reference 186).

176. "Other Resources: A Closer Look at *A Bridge to Light*: An Examination of the Religious Teachings of the Scottish Rite Introduction," North American Mission Board [of the Southern Baptist Convention] Web site (http://www.namb.net/resources/beliefbulletins/resources/bridge_to_light.asp). The source is quoting from pp. 112-13 of *A Bridge to Light*.

177. Rex R. Hutchens, *A Bridge to Light,* Washington, DC: The Supreme Council, 33rd Degree, Ancient and Accepted Scottish Rite of Freemasonry, Southern Jurisdiction, United States of America, 1988.

178. Probably because of the large numbers of Christians who have ended up in Masonry, there are sometimes Christian sentiments found, but these are inconsistent with the overall worldview of Masonry. There are also apparently rare exceptions to the rule of not using Christ's name in prayer in the Lodge, as evidenced in the *Masonic Code* of the Grand Lodge of Alabama: "It is therefore proper and in accordance with Masonic law and tenets for a Mason who believes in Christ Jesus to offer prayers in the Lodge in His Name" (*Masonic Code,* Grand Lodge of Alabama, 1963, . 141).

MW179. "Anti-Masonry Examined," Ake Eldberg's home page Web site. (http://home.swipnet.se/~w-29954/Antimas/). Eldberg also claims Masonry is not incompatible with Christianity and that Swedish Freemasonry is even "an exclusively Christian order" (Eldberg, http://home.swipnet.se/~w-49954/English/eperson.html). In this book, we have shown him wrong on point one. However, at the official Swedish Order of Freemasons Web site (www.frimurarorden.se/), no information was supplied that would allow us to analyze his claim as to the exclusively Christian nature of Swedish Masonry.

180. Letter of Gary Leazer to Don L. Talbert of Chattanooga, TN, January 17, 1993, copy on file.

181. The General Grand Chapter Order of the Eastern Star, *Ritual of the Order of the Eastern Star,* Washington, DC: International Eastern Star Temple, 1956, 1970.

182. The following monitors are samples of those that have been used in our research; bibliographic data is supplied as it appears on the title pages. 1) **Tennessee:** *Tennessee Craftsmen or Masonic Textbook,* 14th Edition, produced by the Board of Custodians Members, February 1963; 2) **Arkansas:** *Masonic Monitor of the Degrees of Entered Apprentice, Fellow Craft and Master Mason,* adopted by the Most Worshipful Grand Lodge of Free & Accepted Masons of Arkansas, November 16, 1954, 7th Edition, February 3-4, 1983; 3) **Alabama:** *Masonic Ritual: Grand Lodge of F. and A.M. Alabama,* Grand Lodge of Alabama, 1978; 4) **Texas:** *Monitor of the Lodge: Monitorial Instructions in the Three Degrees of Symbolic Freemasonry as Exemplified in the Grand Jurisdiction of Texas, A.F.&A.M.,* Grand Lodge of Texas, A.F.&A.M., 1982; 5) **Georgia:** *Masonic Manual of the Grand Lodge of Georgia, Free & Accepted Masons,* 10th Edition, 1983, Code Revision Committee: Harris Bullock, Earl D. Harris, James E. Mosely; **North Carolina:** *North Carolina Lodge Manual for the Degrees of the Entered Apprentice, Fellow Craft and Master Mason as Authorized by the Grand Lodge of North Carolina Ancient Free & Accepted Masons and the Services for the*

Burial of the Dead of the Fraternity by Charles F. Bahnson, Assistant Grand Lecturer, Raleigh, NC: The Grand Lodge of North Carolina, 1943 rev.; **Illinois:** *The Official Monitor of the Most Worshipful Grand Lodge Ancient Free & Accepted Masons,* State of Illinois, Adopted 1916; **Virginia:** *Virginia Textbook Containing "The Book of Constitutions," Illustrations of the Work, Forms and Ceremonies of the Grand Lodge of Virginia,* originally compiled by John Dove, Grand Secretary of the Grand Lodge of Virginia from 1835 to 1876 n.p., n.d; **Oregon:** *Standard Manual of the Grand Lodge of Ancient Free & Accepted Masons of Oregon,* January 1, 1975. **In addition:** Rob Morris, *The Freemason's Monitor or Illustrations of Masonry* by Thomas Smith Webb, Cincinnati: Moore, Wilstach, Keys and Company, 1859; Malcolm C. Duncan, *Masonic Ritual and Monitor or Guide to the Three Symbolic Degrees of the Ancient York Rite and to the Degrees of Mark Master, Past Master, Most Excellent Master and the Royal Arch,* 3rd ed., New York: David McKay Company, n.d; George E. Simons, *Standard Masonic Monitor of the Degrees of Entered Apprentice, Fellow Draft and Master Mason,* Richmond, VA: Macoy Publishing and Masonic Supply, 1984.

MW183. "Masonic Statistics—Graphs, Maps, Charts," Paul M. Bessel's Web site (http://www.bessel.org/masstats.htm) [Bessel is an authority for the Grand Lodge of DC in Washington DC and Executive Secretary of the Masonic Leadership Center]; see also "Masonic Membership Statistics," The Masonic Service Association of North America Web site (http://www.msana.com/msastats.htm#us).

MW184. "All Countries in the World & Whether They Have Masonic Grand Lodges," Paul M. Bessel's Web site (bessel.org/countrys.htm) [Bessel is an authority for the Grand Lodge of DC in Washington, DC, and Executive Secretary of the Masonic Leadership Center]; "All Masonic Grand Lodges in the World—except those in the United States." Bessel (bessel.org/gls.htm).

185. "Report on Freemasonry," North American Mission Board [of the Southern Baptist Convention] Web site (http://www.namb.net/evangelism/iev/mason.asp).

186. C. Fred Kleinknecht, *The House of the Temple of the Supreme Council,* Washington, DC: The Supreme Council 33rd Degree, 1988.

MW187. E-M@son Links (www.freemasonry.org/links/); masons.start4all.com (www.masons.start4all.com).

188. Paul M. Bessel, "United States Supreme Court Justices who were Freemasons," 5/21/98. Found at Web site of Edmond (Oklahoma) Masonic Lodge #37 (http://www.edmond-mason.org/education/United%20States%20Supreme%20Court%20Justices%20who%20were%20Freemasons.html).

189. See 172:23-25 for original references.

MW190. "Frank S. Land, the Founder of DeMolay"; "Frank A. Marshall, Author of the DeMolay Ritual," DeMolay International Web site (www.demolay.org/history/people/).

MW191. Carl Claudy, "Order of DeMolay," St. John's Lodge No. 9 F.&A.M. of Washington Web site (www.seattlemasons.org/claudy/demolay.html.)

MW192. Job's Daughters International Web site (www.iojd.org) and other Web sites.

MW193. Fred H. Whitty, "Watch Masonry Grow," *The Royal Arch Mason Magazine,* Spring 1998. Article found on Ncmason Web site (http://ncmason.org/Archive/spring98/WATCH.htm). According to a note on this site, "NCMASON does not speak for masonry in North Carolina, but is a tool for the lodge and members of North Carolina to use."

MW194. "Masonic Religion!??" Anti-Masonry Points of View Web site (www.masonicinfo.com/religion.htm).

MW195. "Statement on Freemasonry and Religion," The Masonic Service Association of North America Web site (www.msana.com/religion.htm//). Cf. reference 206.

   196. Albert Pike, *The Magnum Opus,* vol. 13, Kila, MT: Kessinger Publishing Co. 1992, p. 6, as cited in 168:143.

   197. Albert Pike, *Liturgy of the Ancient and Accepted Scottish Rite,* Part 2, p. 157, as cited in 168:142.

   198. Albert Pike, *The Book of the Words,* Kila, MT: Kessinger Publishing Company, n.d., as cited in 168:183.

   199. Home Mission Board, SBC, *A Study of Freemasonry,* Atlanta, GA: Home Mission Board of the Southern Baptist Convention, 1993.

   200. Respectively, these five references are found in 89:99; 77:258; 35:64-65; 77:342; 77:258.

   201. *The Scottish Rite Journal,* February 1993.

MW202. Kenneth H. Hooley, "A Declaration for Masonic Action," presented November 30th, 1985, A. Douglas Smith, Jr., Lodge of Research #1949, AF&AM, 2000; as found on Paul M. Bessel's Web site (www.bessel.org/images/ads1-08.pdf) [Bessel is an authority for the Grand Lodge of DC in Washington, DC, and Executive Secretary of the Masonic Leadership Center].

   204. Adapted from John Weldon, "The Masonic Lodge and the Christian Conscience," *Christian Research Journal,* Winter 1994. Used by permission.

   205. Adapted from John Ankerberg and John Weldon, *The Secret Teachings of the Masonic Lodge,* Chicago: Moody Press, 1990, pp. 198-201. Used by permission.

MW206. "Freemasonry and Religion," Grand Lodge of British Columbia and Yukon Web site (freemasonry.bcy.ca/textfiles/religion.html).

MW 207. "U.S. National Masonic Appendant Bodies," Paul M. Bessel's Web site (http://bessel.org/append.htm) [Bessel is an authority for the Grand Lodge of DC in Washington, DC, and Executive Secretary of the Masonic Leadership Center].

208. William Alston, article in *The Encyclopedia of Philosophy* (7 vol.), 1972.

MW 209. "The Craft's Attitude to Politics and Religion," Grand Lodge of British Columbia and Yukon Web site (freemasonry.bcy.ca/writings/ politics.html).

Other Fast Facts® Books

Fast Facts® on Defending Your Faith
John Ankerberg & John Weldon
Bestselling authors Ankerberg and Weldon help you sort through the fundamental beliefs of major religions to separate the truth from errors. From the universe's beginning to the reality of life in heaven, this work answers critical questions.

Fast Facts® on False Teaching
Ron Carlson & Ed Decker
Two cult experts combine their extensive knowledge to give you quick, clear facts about 16 major false teachings of today, and others. Short, informative chapters highlight major issues and contrast false teachings with the truth of God's revealed Word. An easy-to-use resource that gives you powerful insights for sharing the gospel.

Fast Facts® on Islam
John Ankerbertg & John Weldon
Ankerberg and Weldon's Q-and-A format explains Islam's beginnings, Muslims' beliefs about God and Jesus, and how Islamic beliefs relate to recent terrorist acts. A must-have for Christ-centered insight into a growing religious and political power.

Fast Facts® on Jehovah's Witnesses
John Ankerberg & John Weldon
From blood transfusions to works salvation, Ankerberg and Weldon expose the unorthodox doctrines and unbiblical teachings of Jehovah's Witnesses. Whether you're looking for specific information or an overall understanding, you'll find this guide extremely helpful.

Fast Facts® on the Middle East Conflict
J. Randall Price
Price provides "insider" information to answer critical questions regarding the current controversies and viewpoints in the Middle East. You'll discover a fascinating timeline of the conflict, a close look at the groups involved, possible scenarios for Jerusalem's future, and handy maps, charts, and quick-reference sidebars packed with solid, factual information.

Fast Facts® on Mormonism
John Ankerberg & John Weldon
Was God ever a man? Were Jesus and Lucifer brothers? From Mormon definitions of traditional Christian terms to their view of the Bible, Ankerberg and Weldon explore the fundamentals of Mormonism and how they compare to orthodox Christianity.

Fast Facts® on Roman Catholicism
John Ankerberg & John Weldon
Covering the Pope's role in the church, Mary's exaltation, and the authority of Catholic Tradition, this book delves into Roman Catholicism to reveal its beliefs and practices and how they compare to God's Word.

Fast Facts® on the Masonic Lodge
John Ankerberg & John Weldon
Find out whether Masonry and Christianity are truly compatible. The authors clarify Masons' claims and terminology, asking: Is Freemasonry a religion? What do Masonic symbols represent? What do Masons teach about Jesus and the God of the Bible? A great resource if you're a Mason who's unsure about the Lodge's teaching, if you're a friend or relative of a Mason, or if you simply want to be informed about this influential organization.

OTHER BOOKS BY
JOHN ANKERBERG AND JOHN WELDON